Copyright © 2024 Biljana (Bia) Dimovski.

All rights reserved. No part of this publication may be reproduced, distributed, or transmitted in any form or by any means, including photocopying, recording, or other electronic or mechanical methods, without the publisher's prior written permission, except in the case of brief quotations embodied in critical reviews and specific other noncommercial uses permitted by copyright law. For permission requests, write to the publisher, addressed "Attention: Permissions Coordinator," at the address below.

ISBN: 979-8-9852054-7-3 (Hardcover)
Library of Congress Control Number: 2024920168

Front cover image by Biljana (Bia) Dimovski.
Book design by Biljana (Bia) Dimovski.

Printed by IngramSpark® in the United States of America.

First printing edition 2024.

InsideOut Press
PO Box 2666
Country Club Hills, IL 60478

www.InsideOutPress.com

To my daughter – my North Star, my shining light, my best everything! You are the most gentle, kind, and wise person I have ever met. Grow and flourish in your beautiful essence and be who you are, always! Thank you for inspiring me every day. There is nothing you need to do or become to make me proud of you—I am already and always proud of you! ♡ I love you, my sunshine. ♡

To my husband – you have been my pillar in ways I never thought I needed someone to be. Thank you for being amazed at everything I do especially this. You are being biased and I'll take it! ☺
I love you.

Contents

Foreword	IX
Author's Full Disclaimer	XIII
Beyond Parenting Styles	XVII
1. Unexpected Path To Parenthood Finding Strength and Purpose Through Infertility	1
2. In Pursuit of Understanding From Observations to Active Parenting	17
3. Building Blocks of Connection How Early Bonds Shape Emotional and Social Growth	31
4. Holding Space Fostering Emotional Security and Independence	47
5. The Gift of Boredom Why Embracing Boredom Benefits Children	65
6. Boredom In A Hyperconnected World Helping Children Move Beyond Constant Stimulation	79
7. Always Start with the Truth Shifting Focus from Materialism to Relationships	93
8. A Call For Change Building Parenting Communities and Policies	103

9. Parenting in the Age of Information Overload   133
   From Online Influence to Informed Choices: We Must Shift Now!

10. My Agile Parenting Approach   147
    Balancing Intentionality and Flexibility

11. Evolving Together   159
    A Framework for Intentional Parenting

12. Parenting on Purpose   177
    The Essence of Active Parenting

Workbook   187

Foreword

I am deeply driven by a desire to create meaningful change in every area of my life. Sometimes, this change means a shift in perspective; sometimes, it represents tangible change. Regardless of the form in which change comes, I welcome it, as it is rooted in the very essence of how I experience and grow. Life has repeatedly proven that everything happens for a reason and that people can change if they choose to. Things can and do go wrong, and I can appreciate the lessons from my mistakes as much as those times when life is just right. I need to pivot, not balance, and through it all, I am meant to rise above because, somehow, every change – big or small – is, in fact, a tool for the better when it is properly understood.

I am not affiliated with any group, entity, or individual. This book is solely the work of my unique personal and professional experiences and the continuous improvement resulting from those experiences. Events in my personal life led me to people, opportunities, and circumstances I once considered far out of reach. Life has humbled me in ways I can only be grateful for. This book is my way of giving back in appreciation and gratitude for the blessings I have received and continue to receive by the Grace of God. I genuinely believe we are here for a reason. Our life mission is first to experience. Then, we can share our experiences to inspire meaningful change where change is needed and to help someone directly or indirectly by sharing lessons we've learned. I know I have learned quite a few lessons along the way, and I now use these lessons as my foundation for connecting and building relationships.

This book has been in the making for a very long time. The fear, self-judgment, uncertainty, and all the emotions involved in writing it have finally lifted because of a tiny realization I have made: If not me, who? And seemingly just like that, here I go.

Author's Full Disclaimer

I cannot overemphasize the significance of bonding with your child during the first two years after birth. I'm passionately serious about it. This critical and sensitive period plays a pivotal role in the child's overall development, encompassing emotional, social, cognitive, and physical growth. The interactions between a child and their mother or primary caregiver during these delicate years lay the foundation for their future behavior, learning, and health. If you're thinking, "Yeah, sure, but not everyone has the luxury of staying home with their kids," I hear you. I fully recognize supporting this option is a more significant problem that needs to be addressed as a community and on a societal and cultural level. But before we can do that, I think it's vital to raise better awareness about this critical issue related to child development and how a primary caregiver's lack of nurturing care affects our future generations. The primary objective of this book is to contribute to the body of literature acknowledging the importance of parental bonding in the first two years of life and parental physical, mental, and emotional presence in the years leading to adulthood. I hope this book pushes the envelope on this topic further.

This book highlights, outlines, and emphasizes the value of mothers or primary caregivers being home with their children, especially during the early years. Additionally, it points out the gap between the value we need to see and the value we get. Where applicable, I will add my personal experiences as a parent. It's important to note here that there is a plethora of content already written, including research, studies, and other personal opinions from multiple researchers and authors on the topic of parenting and the benefits of a focused nurturing environment for children during their early age and a focused support environment beyond the early ages. Should you wish to explore any topic in greater depth, you are encouraged to conduct your research and form your judgments. This book aims not to be a scientific reference but to offer insights incorporating relevant information and an experiential perspective on parenting that may inspire and inform your approach.

Beyond Parenting Styles

Here are a few thoughts on parenting styles before we dive into the book. I don't believe in being boxed into a category based on averages, generalized statements, or stereotyping. I think each parent finds and evolves through their parenting experience. To that extent, many parenting styles are colored and textured by a person's perceptions, reasoning, and experiences. Excluding obvious common-sense moments and abusive instances, who's to say which parenting styles are suitable and which are wrong? Parents parent based on millions of threads interwoven in their path within their fabric of life. You can agree or disagree with how someone parents, but if I disagree with your parenting style and you disagree with my style, that doesn't make either of us bad parents. Just different from each other. You could be my best friend, acquaintance, friend-enemy, neighbor, or anything in-between; we can have coffee together, we can complain about how messed up and crazy this world is, and then have a deep discussion on how to solve for crazy, or we can talk about the latest episode of our favorite show on Netflix. But just because we are different in our parenting doesn't mean I am right and you are wrong, or you are right and I am wrong.

What we can do beyond the proverbial agree-to-disagree approach is set aside, for a minute, expert opinions and scientific research on parenting and share our experiences, our reasoning, our choices, and the life palette that we carry with us as the foundation for who we are as individuals and as parents. I believe the word we are looking for here is connect. I will argue that we are not currently connected. We like to think we are, but our community of parents lacks connection and a foundation for building solid and meaningful relationships. And I'm not talking about stereotypical wittiness about parenthood posted all over social media for no other reason but to entertain and make you feel validated/justified for a hot second. I'm not talking about shallow, fluff comments used as a cover-up for what's really under the surface. No, I'm talking about putting in the effort to connect and join a constructive discussion around our parenting experiences so we can all consider each other and help each other grow as parents significantly within our households and culture. As parents, we must wake up and reconsider our approaches and attitudes toward life. This is not meant to call out any parent for their parenting abilities and skills. But if you consider yourself a great parent, then you should be able to evaluate potential ideas at least to help you become better, more significant. This way, we all benefit because we now understand each other more deeply than when we agreed to disagree or hid behind a social media short/like/comment that falsely validated us.

1
Unexpected Path To Parenthood

Finding Strength and Purpose Through Infertility

Please understand, as you are reading this, that my actual infertility journey was long, complicated, and completely scattered. It would be unjust and nearly impossible to fit the entire unfolding of events into this book, as it serves a different purpose. However, I am sharing here a highly condensed version, highlights if you will, to provide you with enough context so you can understand the role my infertility experience played in the development and shaping of my parenting experience. This is just one aspect, one of the many threads in the fabric of my own life experience. But it's a major one, and as such, it earned its place here in the spotlight. As you read this book, please note that when I talk about lessons learned, I refer to a concept found throughout my work, interwoven in all areas of my life, not just the lessons of my personal infertility experience.

Never in a million years did I expect I would have such a difficult time starting a family. Although eventually, I gave birth to a beautiful, healthy child whom I adore and love unconditionally and immensely, infertility has taught me a few things about life, the first one being that a family can come about in many ways. Some of those ways may or may not align with some proverbial textbook rules; nonetheless, all are equally fulfilling and possible. For me, having children was like a project with only one outcome; it did not involve a detour, especially not one that lasted 11 years. So, saying that I was shocked when I discovered I may never have children is a true understatement. I became angry and bitter, and overall, I was not a very pleasant person to be around. Mostly, I was angry at myself for being angry and angry at God for allowing this to happen to me. I did not get the lesson. In some ways, I still don't get the lesson. But this part of the experience taught me a significant truth in my life journey: being a mother was never my only purpose. I know it is part of my purpose because I did become a mother, and motherhood informs who I am. But being a parent is not my entire purpose. That was a big realization for me. Once I understood my infertility was a tool to help me, not an obstacle to harm me, everything started turning around in my life. But before I realized that, my life took some sharp turns…

For example, I began viewing my once meaningful career as a colossal waste of time. At the time, I was in graphic design and had started my own business. It didn't last long because, at that time, I wasn't motivated to build a successful business. My energy was focused on motherhood. So, after I finished my projects, I closed up shop. I didn't want to work on creative projects because I didn't feel creative; I felt numb. I jumped onto a few career paths until I realized I could never replace my overarching desire to be a mother by immersing myself in distractions. When I eventually stopped running, I realized I would have to acknowledge the real issue first, accept it, try to understand it, and finally build a new life and perspective that would serve me better. Slowly, I started communicating with myself in a way that eventually turned the victim in me into a victorious warrior.

Socially, I also made dubious choices. I started building up walls because my infertility experience was just too painful to share and too overwhelming not to. It took me a very long time to open up. When I finally decided to turn the page, I began rebuilding a relationship with myself, God, and everyone I had pushed away over the years. I learned a lot about true friendship during this time, and I came to realize the one thing I needed while going through infertility was the very thing I avoided – friends; True friends who were there to hold space for me and who were not just showing curiosity in my life affairs. I pushed everyone away in a massive swoosh, including people I didn't mean to.

My journey to reaching motherhood was challenging. The challenge felt even more significant because I have always wanted to be a mother. Since an early age, I have never doubted that aspect of my femininity. For me, motherhood was a given, and I embraced that given. I just expected it to be the central focus of my adulthood. Most of my playtime included playing with baby dolls. As most kids do throughout my childhood, I changed my mind multiple times on what I wanted to do when I grew up, but whatever the choice, being a mother remained my constant. In a way, I suppose that was an anchor for me. Aside from my deep internal knowledge about how much I would enjoy being a mom, I didn't think much of it. ...One day... That one day came, but it didn't deliver as expected. It didn't show up for me the way I was ready to show up for it. It got delayed. Then it got late. Then it became a concern. Then the problem was confirmed, and just for extra kicks, the situation was devastating; it was, in fact, a check-mate moment. I was told my chances of ever conceiving were slim to none (with emphasis on the none). All I remember from that moment is how time stopped. Everything got blurry for a second.

Sound, including spoken words, became distant, like someone trying to say something through a faraway tunnel. I couldn't make out what they were saying. The words were just sound, fading in and out of space. Unarticulated. Dull... And then the pain. The pain that came from every ounce of my body trying to hold on to everything and anything I ever knew to be true of me in the role of a mom to stop my heart from breaking. To prevent my heart from shattering into a million pieces in just one split moment. How? How is that possible? I am here, am I not? I am standing, breathing, and living a healthy life. Everything is functioning as it should. Am I? Here? Breathing... Am I?

I felt like everything around me, the entire world and everything in it was shattering, yet it remained unaffected. Then I realized it wasn't the world around me; it was me, all of me, breaking inside and about to crumble in the middle of the fertility office floor and disappear entirely. To this day, it's one of the most challenging moments for me to talk about and try to describe without sounding odd or awful. I've heard someone once talk about the feeling of time moving in slow motion during moments the brain doesn't have time to process, so it goes to some almost shut-down mode, and it just observes and waits until it (the brain) finally catches up to what's happening. I think some form of that kind of experience is what I experienced. It took time to process and even more time to understand and adjust to my now-to-be usual self and start thinking about options and the decisions that needed to be made alongside each option. Most of the options didn't even feel like options. They felt like imposed solutions to a problem I did not own. I did not create or ask for this problem, yet here I was, forced to consider "options" I didn't want.

Time is a pretty powerful concept. Most people, including myself, associate time with something we chase to grab as much as possible because it always seems we are in shortage. Going through my fertility journey, I learned a different understanding of time. It's something we need to let come to us. It comes to us by nurturing its children - the moments. It took a long time to realize this; sometimes, I must keep reminding myself. When things don't work out or don't go our way, we need to give time a fighting chance and start with one of its children closest to us, the moment we are in - that one. Things begin to look much more manageable when we only consider the moment now and then the next and then the next. I went through infertility for 11 years. Most of those years were a roller-coaster ride I never wanted to go on. However, they were also filled with lessons I collected that helped me become the person I am today, the mother and wife I am, with all the good, bad, and everything in between.

People say that our circumstances don't define us. That may be true, but it would be ignorant to think that our circumstances, that the events in our life, do not affect us and do not shape our mindset and, by extension, our character — because the choices we later make are all influenced by these very experiences and our interpretation of their meaning in our lives. But, for some of us, what's painfully true and, at times, extremely difficult is that there are always multiple options in any situation in life, and we care for none. Why? Because we are fixated on what we want and can't even fathom what it would be like to consider anything else. The struggle is finding it within us to accept our options (or perhaps to create new possibilities) and adjust our thinking to navigate the storm and come out on the other side in one piece. At least, this was the struggle for me. How dare life not fall in line with my plan of execution!

For me, infertility meant war. And I became a soldier. I went to war with infertility. It lasted for a few years until I realized

I was at war, not with infertility but with myself. That was a much-needed slap in the face, and, for the first time in a long time during my infertility journey, I decided to take the blow for what it was and not react to it, not try to shake it off and keep punching. That was an eye-opening moment; out of the countless calls, the one I answered. Why? What was so special about the realization that I was at war with myself that was not obvious from the beginning? The level of disappointment, pain, and anger that built up in me at the very moment I was told I should probably give up the idea of having children. It's funny how much anger a person can feel without even realizing it. It's double funny the overwhelming emotional chaos and eventual release a person can feel from self-realization. Nothing will ever change for a person until self-realization happens, which is almost immediately followed by a decision to change. Realization without a decision to act is nothing.

Looking back at that time, I feel everything I went through was needed at that time and almost necessary for me to experience to arrive at the destination I did. We all experience different things differently. We all need to experience in a way that serves us. Unfortunately (or fortunately), for whatever reason, we are not aware of that while going through the experience until such moment in time that we are not only ready but also willing to accept our experience for what it's trying to teach us. For what it's trying to teach us, not for what it is. That's because there is a difference between accepting something and accepting something with an understanding of its purpose. We can accept our experiences and continue as we are. Or we can accept our experiences and understand what they are teaching us so we can take the lesson and implement it in a way we move beyond our struggle and into a better way of being. That's the decision part

I mentioned earlier. Realization without a decision for action is a missed opportunity.

My experience with infertility is different from anyone else's. Yes, looking from the outside, it can be summed up as 'hard' to go through, but how each woman navigates through the 'hard' is different. My 'hard' was filled with very intense emotions. When I say there were moments I felt like I wanted to get out of my skin, I'm not exaggerating. I believe the day I was told my hormones were not going to make me a baby, I cried (correction, sobbed) more in one day than most people do in the course of a lifetime. An experience of this magnitude inevitably affected and shaped a good portion of who I am today, how I build relationships, and how I show up in life. I can't change that I was affected by my infertility. I can't change the fact that going through infertility for 11 years changed me. What I can do is choose what I do with all of that. Decide the direction moving forward. My fertility journey has shaped who I am today, which is a different person than I would have been had it not been for the pain, struggles, joy, laughter, sadness, liveliness, and a boatload of emotions I experienced throughout a decade on a single topic! There are lessons we learn and lessons waiting to be discovered. The lessons waiting to be learned are on repeat; keep cycling in our life until we are ready and willing to learn and apply them. The whole point of learning our lessons is to avoid retaking the same wrong turn, but that doesn't mean we will not make new wrong turns farther down the road. My lessons have helped me be a more vigilant, active, present parent. However, those lessons have not prevented me from making the same or similar mistakes as a parent as the next mom. I have had a lot of time to think about what motherhood would mean to me before becoming a mother and use that as my North Star so that every time I mess up, I have my North Star guiding me to get up and try again. This time, try better. Maybe even fail again, better.

Motherhood is not a project you plan and execute. Heaven knows I found out the hard way! Motherhood is a lifestyle you must be willing to commit to and continuously find ways to improve and pivot on a moment's notice. You have to be all in. Especially if having children is a choice you make. In my most challenging moments with infertility, I did something I later identified and called a 'personal temperature check' – not the one you do to detect ovulation time – to check with myself if I am staying true to the 'why' in my pursuit of becoming a mother. Each time I did one of these checks, I was making sure my why continued to be my love for everything involved in caring for a child, guiding my child through discoveries and growth, and building a meaningful relationship with my child along the way. Having children cannot be because it is what society expects, or because it's what the family expects shortly after a couple gets married, or because it's what you do after you get married. Having children must be based on something beyond temporary excitement and novelty. It must go deeper. Motherhood is a blessing we've been graced with. As such, it becomes second to none on your backlog - each time, every time! When I became a mom, everything else became less of a priority. Some do not agree with my approach. That's ok. Some ask me why I take this approach. That response usually comes from parents who highlight the importance of mommy time (personal time away from your child/children). I don't dispute that, but I don't share the same opinion. However, I respect those who ask me why motherhood is my second-to-none item each time. My response is that my why behind motherhood, although personal, is solid and intentional!

The first three months of my pregnancy were, by default, emotionally and mentally in constant conflict. On one side, I didn't want to tell anyone I was pregnant until I was well into my pregnancy for fear of something going wrong and then having to go back and update everyone on the news, thus experiencing all over again the pain of yet another failed attempt. On the other side, excitement was literally past the line of ready and right between the lines of set and go! Even after 11 years of month after month of disappointment, I somehow still had the emotion called excitement alive in me and ready to express itself. All my body had to do was be pregnant. How easy and simple that sounds. For that time being, however, I had to do something that was potentially very much contradicting to any advice anyone would give to a woman expecting a child, which was to suppress my excitement. I've heard of suppressing anger, which is unhealthy, but how about suppressing excitement? That caught me by surprise! But that's precisely what it felt like I needed to do then. You are right if you ask yourself how that can be helpful, healthy, or even needed. I asked myself the same question. This is where the fear came as a useful tactic that helped me navigate through the three months of complete uncertainty and not an ounce of guarantee that this time it would work - that I would get and remain pregnant for a full term.

In previous times, I would get excited thinking that was it, and it would turn out to be a false alarm. By this time, I was wise enough to know better yet aggravated sufficiently to want to hurry up and wait for another month in complete uncertainty. The fear of going through yet another disappointment over something within reach but never in my reach was more significant than the need to shout out to the world that I did it; I finally did it! I got pregnant. So, the alternative was to suppress the excitement. I didn't want to admit that's what I was doing because it sounded so odd, so out of sorts, but the only way to liberate myself from whatever trap I felt I was in was to be utterly and brutally honest with myself. I always believed that, and I always stand by that. No matter how terrifying the truth is, it is the only stable ground I can count on repeatedly.

I acknowledged that suppressing excitement, much like anger, is not the ideal way to handle a challenge, and it can backfire if done long enough. For someone like me, three months of feeling afraid to express my excitement about this pregnancy was a very long time. Instead, once I acknowledged my truth, immediately after, I decided to redirect my mindset toward something that could support my efforts and increase my chances of the desired outcome. I initiated daily internal monologue with my to-be fetus. (Lol) Yes, as crazy as that sounds, I started talking to my uterus. It was the weirdest thing I had done to date at first. As the days went by, it became close to second nature.

I continued my monologues with my unborn child all through the nine-and-a-half months of my pregnancy. Eventually, what were monologues with my uterus turned into dialogues with my child, and nine years later, these dialogues haven't stopped. When writing this book, my daughter is eight and a half years old, and our dialogues are the absolute number one priority of the day. Also, they cannot be short, dismissive, Q&A-like conversations. No. We have at least one educational, life-related, learning-infused dialogue daily. The fun part is that this is not scheduled or forced. It simply happens daily.

Throughout my pregnancy, one of the things that I found helpful and therapeutic was giving a specific purpose to my commute to work. My commute to work was over an hour, and I was mostly stuck in traffic. It is not a pleasant experience to have daily unless you find a way to make it somewhat less frustrating or embark on a mission to make being stuck in traffic fun. How do you do that? Well, if you are pregnant, you could… say… talk to your uterus. Every day between the hours of 7:30 am and 9 am, on my way to work, I spoke to my unborn child. At first, it was primarily things like stick with me, little embryo; I got you, my little one; I've been waiting for you for a long time, so stick with me; you are in the right place, etc. Later, in the upcoming months, it was first reaffirming things like I still got you, I'm still here, we're in traffic still, but that's okay, I got you, etc., and then talking about all the fun things we'll do together, places we'll go, things to learn about life, etc. Some of these talking sessions were emotional, others were funny, yet others were all about how we need to prioritize things in life that are age-appropriate. Yes, I recognize how unsettling this may have appeared to a person (also stuck in traffic) in the lane next to me. Once I got past the three-month "trial period" of my pregnancy, I was determined and ready to give this child of mine the best of me! Defining what the "best of me" means later proved more complex and complicated, especially from my child's perspective. Still, since my daughter was born, I am continuously improving the "best of me." I continue to show up for her every day, to win/fail/pivot/fail, and to continue to improve my approach and style as a parent and mother. And I genuinely love every excellent, not-so-good, and flat-out challenging minute!

The first year of motherhood was all about bonding with my child. I made a challenging decision, but it felt right and liberating by its measure. I decided not to return to work and stay home with my child for that first year. I have profound gratitude for being able to stay home with my child. This society doesn't truly recognize the importance of mothers or primary caregivers staying home with their children for the first year of their child's life. In theory, we are seemingly moving forward by highlighting trend-setting organizations that allow flexibility when starting a family. But they are too few and far between. Although it is nice to recognize leaders who initiated such forward-moving changes, and although it is essential to bring such organizations into the spotlight so we can create awareness around such initiatives, really, on a societal scale where it would make an actual difference, we still fall flat when it comes to fulfilling this idea as soon as corporate rules and regulations enter the conversation. Maybe rules and regulations need to change.

My workplace at the time offered I stay home for an additional six weeks, but after that, my leave time would be considered 'exhausted,' and I would have to go back to work full-time. Twelve weeks. Twelve weeks for nine months of carrying a child is not enough to bond meaningfully. It is just enough time to establish a structure and schedule but not enough time for the child or mother to maintain such a schedule. Instead, drastic change follows what was established as a routine that interrupts everything in an infant's life, and the seed of instability is born. I wasn't going to have it. It was hard, primarily financially, but I said no, I'm not returning. I felt at the time, and I still feel the same today, my child's life as an infant was me. I was all my infant felt, smelled, heard, and saw. Imagine your child just got to this new world and is just establishing some normal that is way different from where they resided previously (aka, your uterus) when a brand-new wave of change just gusted over them. Sure, children can adjust quickly, and at times, we may not give them enough credit for their resilience, but no one in this world can make a convincing argument that 12 weeks is enough time to bond with a newborn baby. Mothers in our society constantly face this challenge, and most have no option but to rely on some form of childcare. Caring for your child also means providing for them, which involves making enough money to meet their primary needs for food, shelter, and clothing. Single mothers suffer double the challenge.

I feel blessed that I was able to stay home with my child for almost four years. It angers me that, on a societal level, this time at home required a conscious decision that dramatically diminished my family's financial profile. The fact that I was put in a position to have to choose between staying home with my newborn child, fulfilling my innate desire to be my child's full-time caregiver, or going back to work to fulfill my duty to provide by spending most of my day away from my newborn working in a corporation that knows me only by employee ID. Although it was a choice that made a dent in our financial area, for me, it was the easiest decision I ever made. I decided to fulfill my innate desire to be my child's full-time caregiver, to take my time to raise my child to guide and teach and help her become a good, kind, respectful human being. That doesn't happen at birth. That happens slowly, over time, with patience and by being present with my child, not by clocking in and out so I can feed her, clothe her, and watch the rest of the time slip away in having to be away from my child. But many mothers (and parents, for that matter) don't have viable options for raising a family. That makes me angry and sad at the same time. Of course, some women don't want to give up their careers; they want to choose both to grow in motherhood and the vocation of their choice. That's different because, in most cases, those women can stay home and be financially stable but choose to split their time. That's a different topic for a different day (or book?) because those women can choose, and they do. Many women want to stay home but can't because that would mean the difference between having dinner at the table and not having one for the day. That is what angers me. We live in a first-world country. All mothers should be allowed to stay home with their children for at least the first year of their child's life and not be penalized for taking that time by losing their seat at the corporate roundtable.

Being able to stay home with my child has been the second biggest blessing after having my child. Taking that time to watch her develop every move, every facial expression, every discovery of the world around her, every little thing she would point at as though asking: Have you seen this? Did you hear that? Have you touched this? This is awesome! Have you noticed all this around us?? As though questioning why I'm not just as excited and just as amazed as she is at all these things put in front of her by life. It was during this time, during the first year with my child, that I started realizing the beauty in re-discovering and re-experiencing the most fundamental concepts of life. I started re-experiencing the beauty in things we take for granted, things we once thought of as entirely new and exciting, exquisite, intricate, and unbelievably fantastic, like the wind moving the leaves on a tree. You don't walk around as an adult thinking about how the wind is moving the leaves on that tree you just passed by. But in spending time with my child, I started having a renewed appreciation for this wind-moving leaves business as soon as my baby abruptly pointed to the leaves with an equally abrupt eureka expression on her face. That's real. That's what you need to be a part of as a mother and be allowed to do so without feeling like you are shortchanging your child by not putting in the hours to make enough money to make ends meet! That shouldn't even be on your radar as a mother. You are raising a child. That's serious business!

2
In Pursuit of Understanding

From Observations to Active Parenting

From a bird's-eye view, life is simple and can be lovely in its simplicity if we stop chasing knowledge and start embracing understanding. But we don't do that. We don't go for a deep understanding of concepts and people as we could because we are too busy absorbing the latest information updates that keep updating. We don't have time to fully contemplate and 'understand' because we chase to 'know' information, so we don't have to fear missing out on anything. Once we absorb whatever we are after, we move on to the next thing because we think knowing is enough. We believe to know is to understand. It's not. We think being "in the know" is where it ends. Being in the know only satisfies our curiosity. That's it. So, when we keep 'knowing,' we keep adding items we come across to a backlog in our mind, and we keep doing that until the backlog starts running out of space. Our mind is running out of capacity to process and prioritize appropriately. It can be immobilizing, and it's called being overwhelmed, but hey, we know stuff!

Over the years before becoming a parent, I have had the opportunity to observe a lot of parents and their different parenting approaches in my role as a babysitter. Observing parents' interactions with their children was something I always found myself drawn toward. Growing up in a large family with many cousins, some older and others younger than me, has primed my caregiving inclinations. As an older cousin, I loved watching over my younger cousins. I always loved being around children, and I always had that instinct (or whatever you may want to call it) that guided me in being more naturally aware when I was around little children. Without anyone directing me, I always felt a little radar activating whenever I was around my younger cousins, allowing me to split my attention between what I was engaged in at the moment and what the little cousin over there was doing. In retrospect, it's interesting how my brother, seven years older than me, always looked after me, and I always looked after my younger cousins. So maybe that instinct I just mentioned is not specific to me. Perhaps we all have it, but it only comes across if nurtured, much like many things that need to be nurtured to grow. I was raised by both my parents and my older brother. I was the baby in the family. Without a doubt, I had a great childhood, and I didn't think much of it growing up and well into adulthood.

I didn't think much of it because it was the standard for that time, that age, that culture, and it also made sense. I grew up in Eastern Europe. Most children were raised by their parents and grew up with their grandparents nearby. The concept of babysitting was pretty much non-existent. Coincidentally, when I moved to the United States with my family, my first job was babysitting. I loved it. I fell in love with the family and loved their kids like mine. On the first day on the job, I took one look at those two cute little faces, and I was overwhelmed by this newfound sense of responsibility. I was 19 at the time. I thought I knew what responsibility felt like. This was different. This was whatever level of commitment I thought I knew, times two! Being a babysitter felt like the most fun and challenging job because, as a babysitter, those kids were my responsibility and my number one priority for a designated number of hours. For the designated number of hours, I was to be with them instead of their parents, not in addition to their parents. It felt a bit scary and motivating at the same time. But mostly, I felt honored. I am honored that these parents, who had never met me before, had one conversation with me and felt comfortable enough to leave me in charge of their two children two to three times per week. Years later, as a parent, I have even deeper appreciation and gratitude for their decision.

I love kids; I always have. As an older cousin, I loved playing with and helping around with my younger cousins. For some reason, adults have always been comfortable letting me watch over younger kids as far back as I can remember. As much as I loved my job as a babysitter, I often questioned why people hired others to watch their kids. I was a part-time babysitter. Some people worked as full-time babysitters. Technically, many children spend more time with their babysitters than their parents. It took me a while to get used to this concept. I wondered why grandparents were not babysitting the kids.

I asked myself questions like, why are families not close together? Why is building a successful career, although important, done at the expense of shortening the time parents could spend with their child/children? Yes, at age 19, I pondered those questions all while meeting new people, partying at times like there was no tomorrow, and moving my way through college while making sure that when I wasn't doing any of these things, I was fully present, focused, and one hundred percent responsible for two small children during the hours designated to care for them, to babysit them. Although I didn't realize this then, those days, that time of my life, provided the foundation upon which I started building my perspective on parenting and what I thought and felt parenting could look and feel like for me when that time came. Fast forward about a decade, I discovered that just because you are the best person for the job, you don't always get the job. Sometimes, life likes to throw curveballs you never asked for or expected. That curveball for me was infertility.

Going through infertility while watching family, friends, acquaintances, and even strangers evolving into their roles as parents led me to dive deeper into the topic of parenting. While waiting for my turn to be a mother, I spent a lot of time (a decade's worth of time) on the sidelines observing, longing for something I never had (at least not yet at the time), feeling excitement for all the big and little things that go along with motherhood that I would one day experience. Anyone who has gone through infertility understands saying 'I went through a lot' is an understatement. Interwoven within all my experiences and events and all my attempts at ending my infertility, including Eastern and Western and all-stern medicine approaches, were my most desired dreams and hopes of becoming a mother. Most all other dreams and plans I had started to fade away in the face of infertility. Infertility, it's a tricky one that one. It's not a life-threatening event, yet it threatens to take so much from your life. And the longer it stays, the more it takes. But as they say (I don't know who 'they' are, so don't ask me), hope is the last one standing! Hope delivered. Through hope, one thing my heart and soul held on to through all hail and high waters was that should

I be blessed with a child, I would ensure she has a childhood as I did. And if need be, I would die on that mountain, ensuring my child knows childhood. I promised myself I would not deliver my child to a system, to a society that is progressively ruining and shortening the childhood years in the name of progress and fun for all the wrong reasons. If need be, I will die on that mountain, protecting and shielding my child for as long as I possibly can from a world headed for what I see as organized chaos and silent destruction. I quit my job once I had my child so I could set the foundation for her childhood. I stayed home with her for the first three and a half, almost four years, so I can set that primer for her always to have a center to come back to as she grows up and finds herself lost in this wild world we live in because I know she may find herself lost for a while. When I returned to work, I worked (and still do) from home to have the flexibility I need to ensure my child comes first. I did this so she would have her foundation and center to return to. And that is the best I can do as her parent and mother. The rest is pretty much in God's hands. I do realize that. As hard as it is to trust everything will be okay, I am fully aware that I am not in full control of anything. However, does that mean I throw in the towel and hope for the best? No! Not at all. I will continue to do my part in actively parenting my child and helping anyone interested in joining me with their children. Infertility took a lot from me, but interestingly, it also provided something quite remarkable. It taught me my why, which set the foundation for the parenting framework I came to develop for myself and my child. It's important to note here that this framework was not premeditated and set on intention. It became a result of my passion to make the relationship with my child my number one priority. I am not suggesting that other moms don't prioritize their children, so please do not misinterpret and construe my words. I am saying that I had decided that, if blessed with a child, the relationship with my child would be my North Star in my life. Everything else would become secondary. That was the most fulfilling decision I had made before becoming a mother. During my entire pregnancy, I talked to my child. I talked to her throughout each fruit size she went through while in my uterus. I told her about how long her father and I were waiting for her, how excited we both were, especially me (I have to emphasize my involvement, of course); I sang to her (I sound so awesome while driving or in the shower, it's shocking I haven't been discovered yet), I covered life philosophies, affirmations, prayers, and gratitude, and of course, always told her how much I loved her and couldn't wait to meet her. On her nightstand, she still has a little art piece that says, "We loved you before we even met you." I wasn't going to wait until she was born to start building that relationship with my child; I was on it as soon as my pregnancy was confirmed. I made my uterus such a cool and potentially entertaining hangout place for her that she didn't want to come out. She was two weeks late, and it took 20 hours in childbirth labor to get her out so we could finally meet her. Beauty and perfection take a whole new level and meaning the moment you see your child for the first time. For a moment, everything stops, and it's just you and your child. Nothing matters, and everything is perfect. Everything is calm momentarily, and all sound dials down to zero except your baby's voice. It's the most breathtaking moment. I remember my doctor and three other nurses, plus an assistant, were still working on sewing an incision that needed to be made on me to pull my baby out, as it was getting dangerous to wait any longer for her to come out. Still, at that moment, the moment I saw my baby, I just said, "Stop! I want to hold her first. You can sew me after." That must have been funny as they all started laughing. At the same time, the main doctor did whatever magic doctors do to temporarily hold an open cut from losing too much blood so I could hold my baby for just a minute before they finished sewing the incision. I knew right then that my baby girl just made that hospital room the most beautiful place on Earth. And she continues to rock my world (and shake it at times) in the most amazing ways. I love you, my sunshine!

I'm not the parent who read all the books on new parenting and what to expect when you are expecting. I don't think I've read a single one of those books. I was expecting my baby, and that was what mattered to me. That was all. Don't get me wrong, I love books. I read a lot—just not those books. Also, I think those books can be helpful for many women. I didn't feel the need myself. It doesn't mean my take is right or wrong. It's just my take. My focus was one hundred percent on bonding with my child in a way that felt right for us. In other words, I knew those pregnancy and new parent books would stress me out, and I've accumulated enough stress during infertility, so I wasn't going to add more. Aside from discovering my embryo's fruit stage during each growth stage, I didn't want to focus on anything else but enjoying my pregnancy. I was blessed enough to have an easy pregnancy.

Hearing other moms discuss those books and reference them in conversations sounded a little too mechanical. A little too 'by the book.' I am a big believer in working around a framework, but I do not believe in checkboxes, and that's the impression I got from observing other moms with these books – lots of checkboxes. I kept getting an overarching notion of doubt and second-guessing from some of these moms, which made me uneasy. So, instead of following a script, I went off-script with my child and felt great about it. During those first few months and into the first few years of my child's life, there was a good amount of adjusting, discovering, and simply enjoying the bonding process as we got to know each other and developed our mother-daughter relationship. This was a blessing I am forever grateful for, staying home with my child during those crucial years of her life, actively observing and creating space for each other to grow in our role – my child as a person and me as a mother.

One of the reasons I believe being present as a parent and actively observing a child during the early years is that everything is novel to them, and to some extent, their novelty is novel to the parent. Let me explain. It's not a novel idea that when a baby first enters this world, everything about their surroundings is new, and it would take time to begin making general sense of everything and even more time to start understanding things on a deeper level. That's nature-intended, thus the need for an actively present parent. The only thing a brand-new baby has going for them is instinct, intuition, and sense. Mom feels familiar, so mom is my safe comfort zone. This means as babies, we start with a clean slate. It is up to the person in charge (aka mom/caregiver) to set the foundation for the newborn baby's world. If you think about it, it's pretty nerve-wracking being responsible for a brand-new life that way. No wonder, as mothers, we are naturally inclined to adopt guilt as a permanent state of mind. We are guilty that we are doing this when maybe we should be doing that for our child or doing that other thing when we should have been focusing on this thing over here the whole time. It's a vicious cycle that is hard to break if we get too deep. Let's look at the concept of setting the foundation for the world our child will experience as an opportunity to collaborate and build something beautiful with our child. The burden becomes the incentive. I will cushion here to be careful not to misunderstand what I just said. I am not suggesting that a child is a project that should be developed into a mini version of the child's parents. Not at all. As parents, we are in charge, but the value is in the collaboration, not in the "in charge" attitude.

When my child was born, I was excited about everything we would discover and learn together. This included things I would relearn or even rediscover about myself through my child. Speaking to my child to teach her and speaking to help her understand, although both involve conveying information, differ in focus and approach, and each has its designated moments to shine. If I talk to teach my child, my primary goal is often to impart knowledge or skills. This may even come quickly to me as a parent because this is an approach most of us are familiar with, as we have experienced it during our formal education years. The teacher or instructor provides information to a group of learners. The emphasis is on delivering structured content that may involve rules where the outcome consists of setting expectations about a particular topic and the behavior I expect of my child the next time the topic comes up.

For me, the teaching approach comes up full speed when safety is a concern, especially when there is not much time or needed level of maturity to go into deeper discussions that lead to understanding. For example, standing right next to me in a public place is a rule I have set with my child since she was a toddler. The level of maturity to understand the why behind that rule at age two is simply not there — just that it's mommy's rule, and we follow it. I get full-blown teacher mode and lay down the rules in such instances. I bust out should-s and shouldn't-s like nobody's business! In those instances, I need my child to know and remember the rules even if she doesn't understand them until she reaches a level of maturity sufficient to understand the rule(s).

On the other hand, speaking to my child to help her understand is more focused on facilitating comprehension and promoting clarity. This approach is much more helpful and applicable in various contexts involving my child and the social environment she experiences daily. The same rule from earlier became more about understanding a couple of years later when I had an age-appropriate discussion about why it's crucial to stay close to me when we are in public, especially in a crowded place. Speaking to my child to help her understand enables her to problem solve and even practice and transfer her knowledge to her peers. The emphasis here is on tailoring the communication to my child's level of maturity.

The tools I find most useful in tailoring my communication with my child consist of many examples and questions. While waiting for the biggest blessing of my life - becoming a mother - I spent a lot of time thinking about how I would collaborate with my child instead of dictating while maintaining a healthy balance between piloting and co-piloting as a parent. I never saw myself "teaching" my child how to become a mini-me. I also never saw myself pushing my child to accomplish things I never got to or could not accomplish. From the very beginning, the biggest prayer I had, next to having a healthy baby, was to be given the courage to go against the grain if I need to when it comes to raising my child and the wisdom to recognize humbling moments when I will indeed need to learn from my child so I can show up for my child in the most beneficial way. I remember one instance in particular when I learned a lesson in an attempt to give a lesson to my child. This was around the time she was three years old. I attempted to bring up the fuller version of the stranger-danger conversation a little too hard. Yes, I may have missed the age mark suggested by studies and research because, as a mother to my child who has spent every breathing moment with her until this instant, I was convinced it was the right time for her to know this. So, I went teacher mode and told her that not all strangers are friendly and not all friendly strangers are okay to follow, especially if they attempt to give you a toy or candy or tell you they will take you to your mommy. I told her this would probably never occur because I would never let her out of sight. Still, in the off chance we got separated, if a stranger offered any of these things to her, she needed to immediately start screaming, start running in the other direction from the stranger, and look for another mom with little kids. I did this in a way that was perhaps too "passionate" for a three-year-old as my child said: "Mommy, can you stop talking? You are making me feel scared." I immediately stopped talking. My first thought was, oh my gosh, did I scar my child for life? But instead of drowning in guilt and panic, I immediately reached for another thought: Wow, at three years old, my child could articulate exactly what she felt with complete clarity and honesty. I must be doing something right. Not everything! I mean… Out of the blue, I just managed to freak out my child. So, I paused and switched my approach from telling to bringing her into a dialogue. I asked what part scared her, and she said it was my voice. I realized then that I must've been telling her this with such intensity that only fear could build up. My fear of her ever being in such a situation. I was shocked at myself and was both surprised and grateful that my three-year-old stopped me from continuing to talk. Because I would've kept going, not realizing all along that I would have been harming, not helping her. I would've been instilling my fear onto her for no reason other than me having that fear. That day, I learned a lesson from my child, which wouldn't be the only one. What happened next was that by bringing her into my lesson and allowing her to ask questions about what I told her, I helped her start grasping the concept of stranger danger as important but not something to fear ever happening. This conversation still comes up, but I am mindful of the intensity I bring in with my child. I am grateful for this instance as it helps me navigate many conversations on many other topics with my child. It's how I can be the co-pilot in my child's upbringing. I pay attention to her tune and to how that tune changes based on her development stages. Yes, there are many instances where I am the pilot. Still, there are just as many where being the co-pilot and helping my child understand rather than teach her is a much better way of building a meaningful mother-daughter relationship. The importance of speaking to understand is that it is flexible and responsive to my child's needs. For parents with more than one child, it is adaptable to each child and can look and feel different depending on their personality and how they experience the world around them. One size does not fit all. Each child is a story on their own, and as a parent, I need to be hyper-aware of the level of comprehension of each of my children and adjust my explanations accordingly. I think of this as speaking with my child rather than speaking to my child. In essence, I set out to transfer my knowledge to my child so she can use it as a foundation, a starting point to sculpt the art that will be her personality. This is why I set guardrails with my child, not rules. Because although there may be a few general rules the whole family needs to follow, many of the rules parents set do not work for every child. Actively spending time with your children (especially during those crucial years) will give you the insight and understanding you need to gain for each child, leading to much better communication and much less frustration around your expectations of them. Over the past eight years, I have organically built a set of guardrails that shaped my role as a mother, mentor, and friend to my child. Yes, you can be all three to your child. I am to mine, so I will fight anyone (figuratively speaking) who says don't try to be your child's friend because you'll disappoint yourself, and eventually, they wouldn't want you to be their friend. Maybe. If and when that day comes, we'll pivot. But so far, we're doing just fine.

3

Building Blocks of Connection

How Early Bonds Shape Emotional and Social Growth

It's no news that the earliest bonds formed between children and their caregivers (primarily mothers) profoundly impact children's future psychological, emotional, and social development. The attachment developed through consistent and responsive caregiving fosters a sense of safety and security crucial in exploring the world around them. It forms the foundation children need to build their self-esteem and serves as the primary basis for navigating future relationships with others. Children who develop this secure attachment that begins in the early days of their lives are more likely to exhibit resilience in the face of adversity, healthy levels of self-esteem, and lower levels of anxiety and depression later. However, if this bonding is lacking, it can lead to issues of trust and self-worth, as well as difficulties in managing emotions and forming relationships. Early emotional neglect is linked to increased susceptibility to stress, attachment disorders, and cognitive delays. Of course, not all of this will have the same effect on every child, and not every child will need and seek the same level of attachment.

During my years as a babysitter, I enjoyed observing children in their environment and paid attention to how I needed to show up for each child. Some children required hugs (the more, the better). These were the ones who would run to me as soon as they saw me to hug me. They would pause when playing every so often throughout my time with them to walk over to me and hug me, just like that. Just walk over, hug me, and walk back to their game. It was funny and cute to me. Other children needed to keep their distance, occupy their space, and take some time to be comfortable with me. I appreciated and respected this as well. Most of the time, in my experience, these children were more interested in connecting via dialogue by talking and asking me questions rather than on an intuitive level by checking in with hugs. I didn't think much of it then, but now I know that in each instance, each child communicated to me what they needed from me, the level of attachment they were comfortable forming with me, and how they needed me to show up for them. Years later, and now as a mother, I know the most important thing to remember as a takeaway from that experience is taking my time to get to know my child so I can understand what works and what doesn't work for her specifically. But to get to know my child at that level, I must spend a lot of time with her, observing, interacting, and listening. This is true for any child.

As an extension of observing, interacting, and listening to my child, I do something I call "stop and drop." I call it "stop and drop" when there is something my child is trying to communicate to me, and regardless of where we are, unless, of course, it's a matter of safety, I stop and drop what I'm doing, and I give her my full attention. Now, I don't do this every time she has something to say. Sometimes, I say, "Give me a minute to finish what I'm doing before I give you my full attention." I do "stop and drop" when I hear something in her voice indicating a level of urgency that needs attention now. Spending quality time observing, interacting, and listening to my daughter has allowed me to heighten my hearing senses and have them explicitly customized to her tune. ☺ I find it essential for every mother/caregiver to practice with their child/children. Why? Let's break it down by point.

Stability and Emotional Security
One of the primary benefits of a mother staying home with her child, especially during the first year, is the potential for developing a healthy bond that promotes a sense of stability and security for the child. The consistent presence of a primary caregiver can facilitate this type of healthy attachment by providing timely and consistent responses to the child's needs. This fosters an environment of trust and predictability, which all children need during their early developmental stages. Structure and consistency are not a choice but a necessity for our little ones, and we need to build and hold that space for them during this stage. I created this space for my daughter during her early years as I held her in my arms for hours while she was sleeping. If I weren't holding her, I would put her in her crib and sit beside her, usually reading a book. I tried to stay mindful and did my best not to have electronics too close to her. This was a challenge because electronics surround us, and long-term exposure can harm the human body, so I tried to be intentional about it. For example, I would ensure I put my phone away from anywhere near her or my body while holding her or when she was napping in my arms. I would ensure I was not on my phone or computer if I were next to her. I was very intentional about this, especially for the first six months of her life. Did it make a difference? I don't know. Did it hurt matters? No! Would I do the same if I had the opportunity? Yes. I tried to be mindful and did the best I could not to put electronics too close to my stomach while pregnant. I didn't execute flawlessly, but I was intentional about it as much as possible, given that I worked a full-time, computer desk-bound job while pregnant. Being intentional about this made it much

easier to give my full attention to my baby and bond with her without interruptions or distractions. It is my personal strong belief that being the primary caregiver to my child during this time in this way provided stability and a sense of security for her. It also provided a calm and post-birth re-energizing for me that I would have never experienced had I decided to go back to work. During these early months with my child, she prepared me to show up for her in the coming years more intentionally than I would have had I been in and out of her daily routine.

Emotional Regulation and Social Learning
When a child and mother spend a lot of time together, it opens a whole world for the little one to learn about handling emotions and getting along with others just by watching and copying. It's like they're teaming up right from the start. Kids learn to deal with their feelings by observing the grown-ups closest to them, especially how they cope with stress and emotions. A mom being there day in and day out can offer the kind of help and guidance a child needs as they go through all sorts of feelings—the ups like joy and love, and the downs like frustration and disappointment. This constant, loving support provides ways for children to handle their emotions. This isn't just good for their mental health; it also plays a big part in connecting with others. One of the things I was adamant about with my child was initiating verbal communication from the very beginning and, in doing so, talking to my child like I would to an adult. As I mentioned before, I spoke to my child while I was pregnant. Also, I never used baby talk with my child, and I never let anyone else speak to her in baby talk. I would stop people in their tracks if they started baby-talking to my child. I did sound things out during the first six weeks while exploring and observing her reaction to sounds, but I didn't communicate with her in baby talk.

Language Development and Cognitive Growth

Children's emotional and psychological development is closely linked to their cognitive and language development. Staying home with my child created more opportunities for verbal interactions, storytelling, and reading activities. These interactions enhanced vocabulary and communication skills and stimulated my child's cognitive growth by encouraging curiosity, critical thinking, and problem-solving abilities. Many times during the day, I would hold my child and walk around the house telling her how excited I was to have her, telling her about all the things I couldn't wait to teach her, to learn from her, to play with her, funny experiences I've had, etc. Whatever I would think of at that moment. Sometimes, I was convinced she understood what I was saying, as some of her facial expressions would match the context of my words. I know she didn't understand, but it made for such fun and cute moments to remember. I miss those moments and often tell her about as many as I can remember. She loves hearing about them. Many times at bedtime, she says: "Can you tell me again about how you talked to me when I was a baby and how you walked around the house with me?" or "Can you tell me about how I would wake up in the middle of the night and you would pick me up and get milk for me and talk to me about how all the babies in the world are asleep, and I need to sleep, too?" And I do; I start from the beginning (again), and I tell her about these moments until she falls asleep. It never gets old, and I love going through the entire memory from beginning to end unless I start falling asleep. Still, there are no shortcuts here. If I miss a part, you can bet I'm being called on it.

Self-Esteem and Independence

The benefit from an enhanced sense of self-esteem and self-worth is derived from the consistent emotional support and positive otional support and positive reinforcement children receive when they spend a lot of consistent time with their mother or primary caregiver. This type of individual attention helps children feel valued and understood, contributing to a positive self-image later in their childhood and adulthood. Of course, while enjoying the security of their mother's presence, children can also be encouraged to explore their environment and engage in independent play. As a parent, I set the foundation my child needs to develop autonomy and self-confidence by constructing this balance between support and independence. One of the things I have been made aware of as a stay-at-home mother is that I'm too involved with my child (aka I'm a helicopter mom), the argument being that I'm not helping my child learn to be independent. I'm afraid I have to disagree with this. As personal experience dictates, eight years into my parenting, my child is more independent than I care to admit! :)

Digressing note: The day my child was born was the day 'I' became 'we.' Until my child started school, wherever I was, my child was too. The only places I didn't take my child with me were stores, restaurants, personal doctor appointments, and hairdresser trips. During those times, I would leave my child with (you guessed it) family, her grandparents. If my parents were not available (that happened rarely), I would cancel or reschedule whatever the engagement. I never had a babysitter for my child. I am not against babysitting – I was a babysitter for years. Also, I am fully aware everyone's circumstances are different. Hiring the right babysitter may be the only option for many parents. That's fine. Most, if not all, points I bring up and experiences I share throughout this book are meant to initiate conversations with another perspective to be considered in deciding what works and what doesn't as you build and sustain your parenting mindset.

Back to where I left my child (with her grandparents): Aside from these places where I saw no benefit for my daughter to be in or experience, I was always with her. If you wanted to spend time with me, you'd spend time with both of us. I made no apologies about that! And I would do it all over again! However, as I spent a lot of time with my daughter, especially during the first four years of her life, I incorporated playdates, time for projects we did together, and time for projects we did separately. I have created space for her to grow with me and grow independently. This was particularly helpful when I started to work again, and we had to start thinking about Mommy's work time versus our time together. We shifted more toward independent activities. It worked well with my new job, as I could work full-time from home. This was a blessing directly delivered by God! I am forever grateful for that! I am aware this is not an option for many women. Maybe this book can contribute to creating enough awareness to change that and make it a standard choice for parents already!

Socialization and Peer Interactions

I am not oblivious that while the home environment offers numerous benefits for emotional and psychological development, it is also essential for children to interact with peers and experience a variety of social situations. This is why, as I mentioned above, I have incorporated structured playdates and participated in some community activities. When my daughter turned three, I signed her up for preschool, where she met more new friends and could practice independence. This was an exciting time and a learning exercise for both of us. I asked the teachers if I could stay with my child during the first two preschool sessions. This was more because I wanted to see what they do so I could decide if preschool, the way it was facilitated at that location, is something I felt would contribute to my child's development in a way that was beneficial to her. Staying with her during the first two preschool sessions may or may not have been the best decision because I made the preschool time separation momentarily harder for both of us. I stayed with the teachers during the first two class sessions. My daughter was aware I was there, and everything worked out fine. For the third class session, when I went in, got her situated, and said goodbye, she didn't like that very much. By staying with her for the first two sessions, I have established "Mommy and I are going to preschool" instead of "I'm going to preschool without mommy." I understood that I would have to walk away from my child while she was screaming for me with her arms extended, reaching toward me. It was the most challenging moment in my entire life as a mother! That day, I closed the classroom door and quietly sobbed for half of the preschool time. The other half, I prayed this would not scar her forever! It didn't. I picked her up, all smiles, running toward me and giving me the biggest hug as she said: "It's ok, mama," like she knew what I was feeling. After that, we had no problem at drop-off. I would drop her off and wait for her in the reception area for a couple of hours, getting some work done on my computer. It was a win-win.

We know by now that cognitive development is most crucial and prominent during the first two years of a child's life. We also know that during this time, the brain goes through rapid development, where neural connections form that are influenced by the child's experiences. If those experiences consist of nurturing interactions in stimulating environments, the child will more easily develop and progress in language skills, problem-solving abilities, and overall intelligence. The little one's brain is a sponge and will absorb whatever water I, as a parent, pour in. On one occasion, when my daughter was six years old, she asked me why I didn't let her watch scary movies that other kids her age had already watched. I explained to her the sponge analogy that her brain is like a sponge, and whatever she chooses for her sponge to absorb, the sponge will absorb and store it in her mind. That can affect how she feels. I told her that putting scary images in my mind would scare me, and I wouldn't say I like feeling scared. She said, "Yeah, mama, I felt scared just hearing what my friend told me; I already imagined what she was saying, and it scared me. I don't want to see what that looks like and have that in my mind."

It can be argued by some research that children who receive attentive care and mental stimulation during early childhood have a better capacity for learning and academic achievement. This foundational cognitive development is crucial for success during the child's school years and beyond, which affects their ability to think critically, solve problems, and adapt to new information. As a mother who stayed home with my child, I have first-hand observed that the combination of staying home with my child along with being actively involved in my child's development has significantly stimulated her cognitive process, including attention, memory, problem-solving skills, and language development in ways that only make sense when done as a chain of events. It certainly doesn't happen overnight. It certainly doesn't happen without trial and error. Perfection is never the key, but consistency is. However, practicing consistency with your child can be challenging, and at times, it can be perceived as controlling by the external world. I have considered the context of this perception as a possibility. After reflecting on it, I found it inaccurate and dismissed it as a distraction to my parenting 'why.' We need consistency to help our children learn and practice from an early age because it becomes much more difficult as they get older. Practicing consistency with my child has never been about imposing and adhering to rules. Instead, it's been about guiding her and providing a space where she can experiment, learn from mistakes, adapt, and persevere. My active involvement with my child has created a chain of events that has positively impacted her development.

First, bonding activities through physical touch, such as holding, cuddling, and skin-to-skin contact, were vital for my child's physical health and development. These interactions provided comfort and security and had direct physiological benefits, including improved immunity and enhanced growth. Positive physical contact in infancy can lead to better health outcomes and lower stress levels. Spending time with a child during physical activities and play supports their motor development, encouraging them to achieve physical milestones, such as crawling, walking, and coordination skills. Being able to stay home with my daughter, I paid close attention to these milestones, never pushing her to meet those milestones, but guiding her and meeting her where she was at each milestone and adding enough elements of support to challenge her but not push her into meeting each milestone before she was ready. For example, I'm happy to report potty training was a breeze. She was potty-trained at two and a half years old within two days. This is not an exaggeration! But it is the result of the work I had put in with her for two and a half years before potty training.

Second, it has enhanced language development by providing her with more opportunities for verbal interaction, including reading, storytelling, and engaging in complex conversations.

These conversations often took place close together. Science has it that these activities not only expand the child's vocabulary but also improve their understanding of grammar, narrative structure, and communication nuances, all touch points that I see my daughter excelling in at school. The constant dialogue helps fine-tune phonetic distinctions and build a robust language framework, which is essential for effective communication and academic success. So far, so good.

Third, it has allowed for cognitive stimulation through play. I have engaged my child in various play-based learning experiences tailored to her interests and aligned with her developmental stage. It's how I learned she is creative, likes to narrate, and loves to solve challenges. It's also how I realized she's good at math but is not interested in the subject; she loves to sing and dance but does not like audiences. These insights have helped me learn how to guide her and show up for her each day, all through play. As I have engaged with my child through play, I have allowed her to explore concepts such as improvisation, cause and effect, problem-solving, and unique connections.

Fourth, engaging her in activities requiring talking and reading from a young age helped develop her literacy skills, which play a significant role in academic learning and stimulate imagination, critical thinking, and language skills. The interactive nature of reading with a parent, such as discussing stories, asking questions, and connecting concepts to real-life experiences, deepens comprehension and analytical thinking. One of our favorite board games that we still play to this day involves a game where we take turns picking objects from a pool of different groups of elements you can use to tell a story once a total of seven objects is collected. The game aims to develop a story on the spot that includes all seven objects you chose from the pool.

On a couple of occasions, I filmed my daughter telling her story. We love going back to watch those videos.

Fifth, providing consistent emotional support and guidance is most beneficial because cognitive development is closely tied to social and emotional skills. Going back to the storytelling board game, asking questions along the way as my daughter would tell her story as well as reacting to different parts of the story as appropriate, I was enabling her to learn how to recognize and navigate social interactions and consider things from a different angle, which would help her later in life to understand and appreciate the perspectives of others. In other words, not everything she would include in the story was wow, excellent. There was that, too, but there was also, hmm, that doesn't make sense to me. Can you explain it again? Or, how about this idea?

Social skills and behavior are shaped by the quality and quantity of interactions a child has with their mother or primary caregiver during this early stage in their development. This is why I believe it's not just about the physical presence when a mother decides to stay home with her child. It's about active, quality time with her child. If a mother stays home during this time but is not fully present and active as a parent, most of these benefits are lost to the child. In most cases, a mother's love is so strong that babysitters and grandparents can't provide the type of caregiving the mother can. Sure, there are cases where family help and babysitting are needed, but this should only be temporary and not a full-time endeavor. For example, some of the children I babysat were past this stage, and my time with them was not dominating their time with their parents. That makes a difference. When a child has one primary adult in the role of a parent, there is a level of stability that is formed that prompts the child to feel comfortable enough to learn and explore the environment around them without feeling insecure or uncertain or having to navigate through different 'parenting/supervising' approaches from each of the various adults in their life. When one primary parent takes ownership during this early developmental stage, children learn faster and grow mentally, physically, and emotionally. Their intellect absorbs faster as they develop. Every child is different, and every child develops at their own pace. However, constant communication through dialogue and interaction helped my child develop language skills more rapidly, which is crucial for effective social interaction.

Other things to consider as a result of staying home with my child are that during that time, I model empathy, we discuss emotions openly, and I encourage my child to express her feelings, contributing to the development of emotional intelligence. This ability to understand and respond to the feelings of others is foundational for building solid and empathetic relationships and navigating social situations effectively. As my child grows and engages in activities with other children outside our home, she practices the social skills she learned at home with me now in broader contexts. As a parent, this became interesting to observe once my child reached her school years. She shares with me school 'happenings' and how she navigated through each happening, and she does this during our daily digests that occur immediately after school, at bedtime or any time in between. This is very important because it gives me insight into her environment when she's not at home, how well she can navigate it, and how I need to show up for her at different times. In our household, 'fine' does not describe your day at school or work.

The development and consistent reinforcement of boundaries I helped my child develop and understand are equally crucial to constant communication through dialogue. This has taught her social norms, which are essential for appropriate social behavior starting from the moment she started school. This is key to understanding the limits of acceptable behavior in various settings. By the time she started school, she already had the foundation for proper behavior away from home. Of course, the foundation will be continuously built over time, but the important part is that it's there.

4
Holding Space

Fostering Emotional Security and Independence

A fundamental aspect of my parenting is holding space for my child. It involves creating a physical environment that fosters emotional acknowledgment and support, where my child feels valued for exactly who she is and how she functions in our collective world. The intention behind this is to remind her every time that her world holds space in the collective world we live in, and it is vital to nurture and grow her world so that the collective world can benefit from her existence just as she can benefit from the collective world. Interestingly, society and culture have hyper-zoomed in on and mastered the "I, me, and mine" approach to life. And we leave it there. I put effort into helping my child understand that it is essential to know her "I, me, mine," but that it is equally important to not only know but understand how to connect that to a network of "we, us, ours" for the greater good because there will be times when "I, me, mine" will need to be put aside and other times when "we, us, ours" will need to take the backseat—holding space in the context of showing up as a parent, friend, colleague, or individual means holding space for that person at that moment and opening space to reach out and do the same for others. This is what I work with my child to help her learn and to practice that it's not always about her or how she shows up for others.

In the last few years, I have noticed a trend where the whole philosophy and attitude toward parenting are focused on "if mom is happy, everyone is happy" or "I need my time and space to be a better mom/parent." Sure, there are moments when these statements are applicable and justified, but I'm observing that sometimes they are overemphasized and misused. I have seen moms tapping a bit on the use-and-abuse side of personal time and self-care, you know, for their children's sake. There was a point in my life as a mother when I felt that because I chose to be fully dedicated to motherhood, I started being viewed as the overly protective helicopter mom who needed to chill and have a drink. This kind of chill attitude toward motherhood/parenthood is often rooted in the belief that first, it is so tiring to constantly be "on" with your child, and second, which is more like a justification of the first one, children need their space to learn to be independent and strong as individuals. I have heard such remarks, and I have not entirely dismissed them because in and of themselves, without additional context, they carry some level of value in their premise. But as is the case with many things in life, especially today, when you pay close attention when you look for understanding rather than just knowing, you begin to see how misconstrued these remarks are from their context. Therefore, what I have done with such statements is to consider them for what they are, remind myself of my why, and then decide whether to adjust my approach or keep walking my talk no matter how against the grain it sometimes goes. I do this with anything thrown my way, but mainly as a parent. To help me stay as objective as I can and make it about learning and improvement rather than personal offense, there are four questions I ask myself every time I need a reset: Is my approach harming anyone in any way? Is my approach adding value to my child's world now or in the future? Will my approach based on a concept that conflicts with mine add more value to my child? Is my approach adding value to our collective world now and in the future?

These four questions help me ground myself and give me the reset I need to continue my parenting journey as I have been or to adjust and then continue my parenting journey with newfound clarity. Regardless of my decision, I am content because I have considered the alternatives instead of immediately dismissing what I haven't considered before just because it's not coming from me. And this is where I see the power of AgileParenting™. It's not about being right or wrong; it's about being content with my decisions. Personally, the times I have regretted a decision (parenting or otherwise) have been when I did not allow myself to consider alternatives. My decision may have been the same, but I wouldn't know because I didn't consider potential options. This happened during my infertility journey.

For years, I didn't allow myself to consider other options for parenthood. Once I allowed myself the space to think, I discovered it didn't matter how I got to my baby because I would love that child regardless. After all, I had babysat for years before I had my child, and I always cared for each child as if each child were my own. Consider. Always consider. That has stayed with me and followed me throughout my parenting journey so far. And in my consideration, I always ensure I exclude how my decision will appear to the external world. In my experience, the external world lives by trends. I don't.

To me, parenting is not a trend. I'm not interested in making myself relevant with other moms. I'm not interested in justifying or apologizing for not agreeing with some parenting approaches. I'm sure a lot of parents don't agree with my approach. However, I always welcome a good, meaningful discussion on the topic. I do not want to convince anyone that my parenting style is correct because I don't know it is for everyone. But I know that by sharing my parenting approach through conversation or putting it in a book, I am offering my vulnerability to you. I invite you to join me in having more conversations about parenting and how to help each other make it better for our children within our homes and make it better for our children within each community. I observe over and over that we need this conversation, and we need it away from social media and public scrutiny. We need communities. We need parenting communities, not by name and status but by values and actions.

I have embarked on this journey by choice. I believe in putting my child first, just as most parents would. I also think that every time a parent justifies a decision based on convenience, they are not putting their child's needs first. A child needs to learn patience over instant gratification. A child needs to experience boredom over constantly being entertained. A child needs to understand that the world isn't going to put them first (and that is okay) over growing up to feel entitled. But for our children to learn all these things, they need to have that foundation built inside their homes so they don't need to search for them in the outside world later.

For this reason, I have made small conscious choices throughout my parenting that each on their own may seem trivial at best, but combined, have made a difference in my child's development. For example, I have not let my infant cry herself to sleep or, as a toddler, turn her away when she would come to our bedroom in the middle of the night looking to be held. I listen to my child. I collaborate with her, and I do it in a way she knows and understands the two roles each of us plays at any given time – for me, the role of a mother and the role of a friend, and for her, the role of a daughter and the role of a friend. She gets it. And that is all I ask for. The rest is about holding space for her and listening to understand her, not problem-solving for her unless she specifically asks for help finding a solution; then, we roll up our sleeves and start problem-solving together. So how do I do that? How do I collaborate with my child so that she understands each of our roles? I let her talk first. I can tell when she has something that's bothering her. I'm sure a lot of moms can relate here. You know when something is weighing down your child. Initially, I would ask her: *"What's going on, baby?"* or *"Is something wrong?"* As a parent, I pride myself on being very direct and transparent with my child. However, in this area – when something is bothering my child – I very quickly abandoned that approach. It took much longer for my child to share what was bothering her when I point blankly asked her what was bothering her than if I created space for her to bring it up herself, taking her own time. Every child is different and responds differently in various areas across their developmental stages.

I discovered that by asking my child directly what was wrong, I was putting her on the spot, making her feel rushed, namely closing the very space I wanted her to have instead of holding it open for her to feel comfortable and ready to share. So, I switched my approach to something that was a bit more challenging for me but worked well for her. As soon as I would notice something was bothering her, but she didn't know how to bring it up, I watched for an opportunity (or create one) where it would be just the two of us either working on an art project or watching something on TV, or being engaged in an activity that does not require deep focus but has us both occupied. Then, I would bring up something I would need her opinion or help with deciding, like what book I should read next or if I vacuum today or tomorrow (the advice was always tomorrow ☺). Then, what would happen next was amazing. Shortly after discussing what I needed help with, she would ask, *"Can I tell you something?"* My answer has always been yes. And then, I would hold space until she told me what was bothering her and what she needed from me – to listen or listen and then advise.

The most critical aspect of holding space for my child is active listening. Absorbing what she is telling me at the time without trying to think of a "good" response or any response. It helps to remind myself that what I'm doing now is listening, not constructing a solution. I'm not going to lie; it's a lot easier for me to stop listening and even interrupt mid-sentence and say something like, listen, here's what you need to do… The irony is in starting my premature response with "listen." As straightforward as it is and as well-accustomed as I am to this kind of communication approach, I fight the urge and focus on listening until the end. And yes, it's a choice – every time! It doesn't become second nature but gets easier as you practice it. Isn't that the case with anything?

I communicate everything with my child. I tell my child she should never be afraid to tell me the truth. I remind her that I will never be upset about what she did, but I will get mighty upset if she chooses to hide the truth from me and I find out something that directly concerns her from someone else. I tell her that no matter how bad she thinks the truth is, it is never as bad as a lie. I know that communicating with my child this way validates her emotions, experiences, and connection to the very bottom of the matter – the truth and everything that comes with it. So instead of dismissing her feelings (you shouldn't feel that way) or downplaying her feelings (that's life), I acknowledge the legitimacy of what she is experiencing at the time and acknowledge that it may or may not be something others experience in similar situations, which is fine. I am building the foundation for her emotional intelligence and self-awareness by communicating with my child this way. This way, she knows what she's experiencing is valid regardless of whether that experience is the same as everyone else's or different from everyone else's. By communicating with my child this way while holding space for her during challenging moments, I am building and nurturing an environment filled with love and support. The intention is to offer empathy and encouragement, empowering my child to find her solutions. This approach instills resilience and problem-solving skills, preparing her for the inevitable hurdles in life. Holding space is closely tied to the concept of unconditional love. It means loving and accepting my child for who she is, regardless of her achievements or mistakes. I pray this unconditional love provides a stable foundation for my child's self-esteem and confidence. I know that self-esteem and confidence come easier for some than others. What I am doing for my child is building a strong foundation for it. She will need to discover her self-esteem and confidence level, but why not give her a head start? This way, my child experiences the level of autonomy she needs at that time while I guide her through that experience. This prepares my child to adapt to unavoidable concepts such as identity crises and peer pressure. For example, recently, my daughter experienced a social struggle with two of her friends. In a few instances, when the two other girls were together, they would team up and avoid my daughter, but separately, they would reach out and want to play with my daughter. This behavior was repeated in a few instances. After the third instance, when I was alone with my daughter, I asked her how her playdate went with her two friends. She said she felt like she was pushed aside when it was the three of them but that when playing with each one separately, she enjoyed playing. That made her feel both sad when it was the three of them and happy when she played with each one separately. I could tell my daughter was confused, so I asked her if she wanted to hear what I thought or if she just wanted to share that with me without further discussion. She paused for a moment, thought about it, and then asked me what I thought and what I would do. First, I complimented her on her ability to make that observation. I told her I observed the same. Then, I told her that her feelings were completely valid and that I would most likely feel the same if I were in that situation. Being completely transparent with my child, I said that I would even feel more angry than sad. Finally, I quickly checked in with her to confirm she still wanted to hear what I would do. After she said she did, I said she could choose whether she wanted to act on this, but I would confront both friends, simply asking them why they pushed me away when they were together. I left it at that and sat in a few moments of silence with my daughter. By nature, I am much more contentious than my daughter, so I knew she might not feel comfortable with this approach, just as she knew I would tell her exactly what I would do. After a few moments of silence, she said she'd think about it. We left it at that. Some time passed, and the three friends didn't get to play together for a while due to other activities. About a couple of months later, my daughter had one of the two friends over for a playdate. After the friend left, I asked my daughter if she had fun playing with her friend. She told me about the playdate, and at the end, she said: "By the way, I asked my friend why she acts differently when the other friend is around, and she said she didn't realize she was doing that, then she apologized and promised not to act like that again." I could see the change in my daughter's attitude and hear it in her voice. She felt proud, she felt heard, she felt valued. At that moment, my daughter felt a level of confidence she chose to reach for. The thing I found most remarkable was that she thought about her dilemma with the two friends; she considered my suggestion, but she made her own decision on the solution. She decided to address the issue with one of her friends, not both, contrary to my suggestion. It's safe to assume she addressed the issue with the friend she felt she needed to confront. My daughter decided how she approached her solution to her problem due to the space I held for her. I didn't tell her what she should do. Holding space is all that's needed. The rest falls into place in its own time and order.

A parent who holds space for their child/children in this way helps them navigate these challenges with a sense of self-assurance. When I have space for my child, I am helping her learn to empathize, communicate effectively, and constructively navigate conflicts. I am confident these skills will contribute to her building healthy relationships and social interactions throughout her life. I want her to learn to trust her abilities and judgment, which is crucial for building resilience in facing life's uncertainties. I feel the effort I put to work with my child on her way to becoming an emotionally intelligent and compassionate individual is my gift to society every time she engages in acts of kindness, empathy, and understanding, thus fostering a community and a world that values connection and support. That is every parent's contribution and gift to society. If we all focus on making this the task and the reward all into one, we will raise generations of people supporting each other rather than competing against each other. This investment in holding space pays dividends in the form of emotionally intelligent, empathetic individuals who contribute positively to their relationships and their communities. So why not make it a top priority? So why not make that giant cultural leap and hold that same space, set that foundation for new parents to provide such a foundation for their children, and not be penalized for choosing to do so? We need to rethink our societal values and priorities. We must stop dismissing individuals and groups that are raising this parenting awareness. We must stop prioritizing corporate profit-making ideas and start prioritizing quality-of-life ideas that are much more sustainable and driven by common sense!

I know parenting one child differs from parenting two, three, or more children. Parenting gets even more interesting because each child has their personality and way of processing thoughts and feelings and seeing the world. So, how you hold space for one child will differ from how your other children need you to hold space for them. All things equal, you need to be there to observe each child learn about them and understand them to the best of your ability so you can hold space for each one in a way that is meaningful and beneficial to each child. That takes time. That takes effort. That takes familial and societal support. This is why small parenting communities are an essential part of this equation. Becoming a parent is the most critical role in a person's life; it's a lot. It is why becoming a parent is not something to check off a list or do because everyone is doing it.

It saddens me to observe parenting today. It saddens me how much we have succumbed to social media and how parenting is portrayed almost as a chore. At the same time, mothers/parents are depicted as overly unappreciated family members because the kids are so demanding. Yet, nothing is done about it aside from posting humorous videos of how difficult, bossy, and entitled their kids are; for what? The comical performance earns a few laughs and likes. All along, I'm thinking, these kids are modeling the adults in their life. So, it seems these adults need someone to hold space to figure things out.

Another notion that saddens me is how, as parents in this culture, we are supposed to "jokingly" long for the days the kids will move out so we can get our lives back. I don't understand that. The very thought of my daughter one day moving out makes me want to cry. I don't ever want her to move out. I also realize she should and will, but I'm not counting the years until that happens. I don't want to even think about it until such time comes. Children feel us. They feel when we are overwhelmed, angry, happy, sad, and everything in between. They feel. They know. I never want my child to feel like she's a burden. When I feel sad, I tell her why I feel sad. When I'm happy, I share my happiness with her. When I'm frustrated, I tell her why. I do this so she never wonders if it has something to do with her. I tell her I love her every day. I miss her when she's at school and can't wait to see her after school.

What I don't do is tell other moms I can't wait until school starts again because I'm just so tired of having the kids at home and need a break. And yes, I can already hear the collective judgment thoughts circling among some of you reading this: Well, if you were in my shoes, if you had to do x, y, z as I do if you had more than one child... Well, I don't. I have one child and will not pretend to understand exactly what it's like to parent five. But one thing I will say, and I stand by (you can fight me on this if you wish), is that becoming a parent, mainly by choice, is a big deal. And it's a big deal not because a brand-new human being has been brought into this world (sure, that too) but it's a big deal because there is a sense of responsibility that goes along with raising that brand-new human being into a decent human being. Contrary to common belief, it is no longer about me and my comfort – it's about me and my child as a unit.

I know how to hold space for my child when I am attuned to her needs. I listen to understand her thinking process, her decision-making process, and her outlook on life. The fantastic thing is that as I try to attune to her needs, she also tries to attune to my needs. I don't tell her she needs to do this; she models it from me. In other words, she learns to understand me just as I learn to understand her. It's not about hierarchy. It's not about control and command. It's not about me versus her. Instead, it becomes about us. That is still missing in our culture, in general, and specifically from the aspect of parenting. Whether we admit it or not, in a culture of "what's in it for me," it's hard to practice and model mutual respect for our children that focuses on the whole. It's hard but not impossible. So, let's make it possible because when you practice holding space for your child organically, it becomes about understanding and respecting each other as a unit. Every child is unique, and effective parenting involves recognizing and respecting each other's differences. Whether it's supporting varied interests, acknowledging different learning styles, or understanding diverse emotional expressions, holding space means embracing the individuality of each child as part of a whole, not as a stand-alone attribute. This acceptance contributes to a positive concept of the self and others and reinforces the idea that the child is valued for who they are because they value those around them.

In times of conflict or challenge, holding space for my child means I build and maintain a delicate balance between offering guidance and allowing her to learn from her experiences. This is easier said than done when I want to give my child all my knowledge by skipping through this delicate process and solving all her challenges simply because I've been there; I've done that, so I carry the wisdom needed to overcome this challenge. The only problem is my child hasn't. Guiding can be difficult. Because you must let the person experience the process even though you know you can make life a whole lot easier for them by giving them the shortcut version. You only need to pull them over to the other side of their challenge – done. Trying to help in this way leaves a big hole in their experience, a void that leads them right back to such challenges the very next opportunity shows up. Instead of imposing solutions, as parents, we need to hold space for our children to explore possible outcomes and consequences. This approach cultivates critical thinking skills and a sense of responsibility. It teaches children that mistakes are a natural part of growth. It teaches them they can do hard things, including navigating challenges with resilience and self-reflection. Guiding my child through daily or weekly self-reflection is one of the most critical skills I focus on helping her master. There are multiple viewpoints on parenting, including dos and don'ts. Still, I am convinced that holding space for my child extends beyond any of those viewpoints, and it strengthens our parent-child relationship, setting a solid foundation for how she sees the world around her. No electronic device can span up content to provide this kind of foundation for my child. Modeling empathy, kindness, and understanding must come from the parents, not from the external world or movies. Done consistently, it contributes to developing a socially conscious individual who is compassionate, tolerant, ethical, and socially responsible – positively contributing to society from childhood to adulthood. Additionally, my intention behind holding space and having an open dialogue with my child from an early age was to encourage her to seek help when needed and early on.

Holding space for my child lets her know I am there for her by showing her rather than telling her I'm there for her. I am showing her that there is nowhere else I'd rather be but right here with her, and I'm showing her that through presence and mindfulness. I am giving her my full attention. Children can tell when you don't give them your full attention. Sometimes, it's warranted, but not during times that call for holding space. Those times call for full attention to be granted to your child because it will significantly contribute to their overall development and well-being. Attention is a fundamental building block in shaping our children's emotional, cognitive, and social capabilities. Attention is what fosters a healthy attachment between me and my child. I ensured I gave my child that attention during the infant stage when bonding was crucial. I make sure I continue to provide that attention to her now when she says: "Can I tell you something?" My intention behind giving my infant 100% attention was to lay the groundwork for building trust and safety in our relationship. That contributed to her cognitive development, creating a conducive environment for learning, exploring, and nurturing her creativity. My intention today, behind giving my eight-year-old daughter 100% attention, is to continue to build on that groundwork I started eight years ago and make it unbreakable.

It's no secret that children who feel seen and heard are more likely to express themselves creatively. This is vital for their emotional expression and the development of problem-solving skills. Giving my full attention during activities such as art and storytelling is simply another way of holding space for my child. Although I didn't think much of it at the time, in retrospect, in my very fresh and early days of motherhood, I established my 'mothering' principles in my relationship with my daughter. Eight years later (when writing this book), I still stick to these two principles because they have repeatedly proven reliable in their simplicity and application.

Establish a solid emotional connection and maintain open and honest communication. Express love and support daily. I actively listen so I can understand and then repeat what I heard to her so she knows my mind is genuinely focused on her. Spend quality time together playing, walking, discussing anything that's on her mind at the time, now that she's older, reading together, journaling, working on projects, etc. Give my full attention right there and then. I don't much care who's around. As long as we're not in anyone's way or disruptive, I level myself eye-to-eye with her and have a chat. Explain. Everything. At any given time. If I'm frustrated and I can't show up for her properly, explain why (in age-appropriate terms), then ask for space for myself until I'm ready to show up for her. She has been able to give me that space every time because she knows how. Believe it or not, my child has hardly ever thrown a tantrum because she hasn't had to. I will digress for a moment here:

The only time my child has thrown a tantrum was at 18 months old in a store at the register. Long story short, she didn't get what she wanted. It was the one time I ignored her cry for attention and focused on nothing else but completing the transaction. I was in the way and was disruptive to people around me (the exception I just wrote about in the list above). I didn't speak to her while she was in the tantrum, I didn't yell, I didn't apologize to anyone around me for my child's behavior. Instead, I intentionally decided to help my child and everyone around me by focusing on the task that needed to be completed or seized, and that was paying for my items. It didn't take long as I didn't have many items. Once that task was done, I walked out of the store and back to my car, my child still in her tantrum. I sat in the back seat with her and gave her space to finish crying. At that point, she was winding down and was more confused about why I was not in my driver's seat than tantrum-y. When she finally stopped crying, I hugged and held her. Then, I talked to her just like I would to an adult. I asked her why she was so upset. I asked her if she thought that was okay, to which she said no; then I explained that what she did was unacceptable and that there were much better ways to express what she wanted. Yes, my almost 2-year-old got it. And she got it because I didn't baby-talk to her. She got it because I treated her with respect – I acknowledged she was upset and gave her space to express that. I know she got it that day because she never repeated that behavior. And at the end of our situation, she said to me in the cutest voice ever: "Mommy, I love you!" We drove home jamming on "The Wheels on the Bus" and never spoke of our little situation again because there was no need.

Encourage independence by showing her she can always depend on me as her mother and best friend. Yup, there it is again. I'm claiming it! Contrary to some beliefs that you shouldn't try to be your child's best friend, I'm going against the grain when

I say I can be my daughter's best friend. I fully acknowledge that there will be times when she will build some distance, just as there will be times when she will pull me in on her challenges. I'm okay with that. By doing that, I will be modeling precisely what a best friend should behave like so she can observe and know who her best friends are. If we show up for the people in our life as we would in our roles as parents, and if we show up for our children the way we once did and still do for our best friends, I think we'd be collectively elevating something quite profound. I always remind myself to model positive behavior to my daughter and remain honest and objective. This is the blueprint I am building for my child to use in her interactions throughout her life.

I know my child's needs will change as she grows up, but I need to adapt my approach and continue to address her attention needs as they grow in and out of intensity and hit each age-appropriate milestone. I will continue to help provide the necessary support and attention that aligns with my child's developmental stage.

5
The Gift of Boredom

Why Embracing Boredom Benefits Children

As a culture, we have grown to frown upon experiencing boredom. Somehow, we have come to experience boredom as an undesired state of mind to be avoided and even mended—a white space to be populated with something, anything. It's interesting how the more we try to fix boredom—to fill in what we experience as a void—the more bored we get. We are focusing on the wrong thing to fix. Think about every time you let your child play with your phone or every time you stop what you are doing to fix boredom for your child, be it by setting up a game on their electronic device, giving them a project to do, or taking them somewhere for the sake of doing something so both you and your child aren't bored. Indeed, children often experience boredom due to various reasons. As a parent, it's essential to understand the underlying factors contributing to this phenomenon. Boredom in children can stem from a lack of stimulation, limited access to engaging activities, or unmet emotional needs. There is a popular belief that this needs to be addressed by producing diverse and age-appropriate activities, fostering creativity, and cultivating a supportive emotional environment. Those are valid steps to consider depending on the underlying reason for the boredom your child is experiencing. However, the focus is on the symptom, not the problem. Boredom isn't the problem. The way we solve boredom is. We need to get out of this mindset that if your child feels bored, you must put a screen in front of them or have something prepared for them to be occupied with. Yes, children get bored when their environment lacks variety and stimulation. However, constantly creating activities for them and having them jump from one prepared thing to another may lead to a different extreme. This extreme happens when that tempo of constant engagement, entertainment, and doing gets interrupted, and nothing can fill that void. This is when children start facing emotions that they are not equipped to deal with. A child is not equipped to deal with these emotions because these are new emotions that need to be discussed instead of avoided. Boredom needs to be practiced in a positive context instead of prevented. Repetitive routines or a limited range of activities can fail to capture a child's interest, leading to a sense of monotony, but only if that child was never introduced to simply being as a separate way of existing from being through doing. As a parent, I have introduced diversity in my child's daily routines, outings, and playtime to the extent of offering options for her to choose from, but only after I have given her ample time to sit in boredom and see what she comes up with on her own as to how to alleviate her boredom. Nine out of ten times, her creativity has prevailed, not mine. She has grown through her creativity each time without my creating and offering options. Boredom is not something to be prevented. Boredom should be encouraged and observed because, during boredom, children practice being great inventors and even discover things about themselves. Let them! It's hard initially because it requires some work and patience, but anything worth doing is hard until you get the hang of it, and then it becomes second nature. This happens from when a baby learns how to get nutrients through breastfeeding, to learning how to walk, to learning how to speak, to learning how to write, to learning a new skill to advance personally and professionally, and so on. Over the past eight years, I have created a playful environment for my child to engage in age-appropriate activities as I understand the importance play has in her development. However, I never did this to combat boredom. I created a playful environment for her because it's a crucial aspect of her development, which is different from trying to shelter her from boredom. Children need access to age-appropriate toys, games, and books that cater to their interests and developmental stages. Additionally, providing children with toys and games as a primary approach to parenting is never the answer. Being actively involved in playing with your child makes children's toys and games beneficial to their development. As a parent, I have been actively involved in my child's life, especially during the early developmental stages. Why? The answer is to select activities that align with my child's preferences, not preferences based on the latest trends in the children's section at Target. One of the first things I introduced to my child was the concept of improvisation. This timeless skill evolves as she ages and can serve her in multiple situations. Involvement in this way helped me foster a sense of excitement and engagement in my child every time she discovered her answers and solutions. It also helped me as a parent to learn about my child as an individual and strengthen our parent-child bond. It allows for creativity to unfold. I consider creativity a key element in my child's personal development. However, over-encouraging imaginative play can backfire and hurt a child's psyche later in life when life expectations don't live up to the standards of the magical world the child was so encouraged to believe in. I know, I know. It goes against some research. Well, this is me going against the grain. I'm not disputing research and studies, but at the end of the day, I am not a statistic, and sure as the sun will rise tomorrow, my child isn't either! Statistics inform and give you a "food-for-thought" awareness for your consideration. They are not the be-all-end-all; plus, the findings keep changing. What studies showed as evident yesterday is proven wrong and overshadowed by new research today. Statistics aren't raising my child. I am! I see my child day in and day out. I know how she breathes. That's why I am her parent and raising her—not a researcher.

I will share something for which I've gotten a few raised eyebrows over the years, but that hasn't caused my child to be any less creative and artistic. My child has known from the beginning that Santa is a fictional character. Honesty is more important than creating a 'magical' world based on falsehoods. While consumerism-driven companies like Disney profit from these stories, children face disappointment in learning the truth later. Many children struggle when they discover that Santa isn't real, and I decided to spare my child from that kind of disillusionment. I encourage my child's thinking process around imagination as just one area in her development. Science is another. Spirituality is another. And they all have a place but are not muddied by magical nonsense. There is a clear distinction between what's real and what's not.

Playing pretend is acceptable for the duration of the game. When the game ends, the pretend ends. You would not see me run errands with my toddler dressed up as Elsa during her toddler years because she thinks she's Elsa. She would wear an Elsa costume at home during a dress-up play, but when it was time to leave the house, she knew she needed to get actual clothes on. She got this. It was not a struggle to make this a rule or anything like that. I would say, let's pause the game because we need to go bye-bye, and she would say: "ok, I-go change." It was so cute hearing her say that. This approach has encouraged her to ask intelligent questions from an early age. I recognize that every child is different, but every child deserves to be met with honesty and truthfulness from day one. I always give my child the truth, followed by an age-appropriate guided discussion so she can develop a level of understanding on a topic that prompts her to think and process information in a way that helps her come to her conclusion.

Before deciding on your belief system regarding boredom, I want to make an important note that I'm sure you already know. Still, I will state it anyway: your child's emotional needs are at play regarding how they experience boredom. Boredom can sometimes manifest as unmet emotional needs, such as the desire for attention, affection, or connection. And this is not necessarily a characteristic of bad parenting. Sometimes, it can be hard to show up for your child in the way they need you, especially if their personality is quite different from yours. For example, I am far more contentious than my daughter is. She's more of a peacemaker. But we are both quite persistent. So that's something to bond over. I fully recognize that my daughter will not be a mini version of me.

Thank the good Lord for that! I don't want to train my child to be like me. I want to do what's called knowledge transfer. I want to offer her all my life tools so she can choose and use them from a pool of resources on her personal life journey to discover and become who she is. Not who I want her to be. Always who she wants to be; this is why I treat parenting a lot like coaching. I guide her through her decisions, but she takes ownership of each decision. So, I guide my child not to be mini-me or some better version of me. No, I guide her to be the best version of herself! That is the measure I'm after. I must be present and involved in her life for that to happen. Not only when I feel up for it but also when it means I 'sacrifice' my comfort. Why? Because I can do that. I'm the adult. I have already developed as a person. I know who I am. I need to help my child develop who she is. It's not about me or my comfort. It's about her. And as a parent, it doesn't feel like a sacrifice. It feels like a blessing. I was given this fantastic opportunity to be a part of something other than myself. As a mother, everything in my child's world until she becomes an adult is my business. And no, not in a suffocating, controlling way. I can almost hear the comments that may arise from this one point I'm making, but I am confident, and I stand by it, that your child needs you to show up consistently, not perfectly! Just consistently and transparently. I tend to my child's emotional needs regardless of how I feel. Sometimes, I'm a hundred percent; other times, my battery is dangerously low. It happens. But the important thing is no matter what, I work it out with her right there and then. If I am irritated, I tell her that; if it's age-appropriate, I may share why. I don't lash out at her because there is something I'm frustrated about that has nothing to do with her. If not age-appropriate, I state what I need at that moment to bounce back. It's usually a moment of quiet and a few deep breaths. After that, I can regroup and address her needs much more effectively. And you know what? Openly stating how I feel and what I need to feel better demonstrates firsthand to my daughter that it's ok not to always be the best at everything, ready for everything, or appear in a particular light. It also demonstrates that it's not ok to dump your baggage onto someone just because you have a shitty day, moment, or situation. It proves that she is my number one priority but that we are all human, and that means attending to her emotional needs doesn't come in the form of instant gratification. Sometimes, she needs to wait a minute.

I am very much attuned to my child's emotional cues and make every effort to create a nurturing environment for her. Part of making that nurturing environment is being open and honest with her. Spending quality time together, engaging in meaningful conversations, and expressing affection make her feel emotionally fulfilled. I always caution that screen time can be a double-edged sword in the age of technology. I don't count this as quality time unless it's a movie night and we're watching something together and making comments together. My daughter had no digital device access until she started kindergarten. She had to do so at that point, precisely due to the pandemic. And guess what! She didn't have the slightest problem figuring it all out. I never gave my child my phone to keep her entertained, not even during our four-hour trips to Michigan to visit family. And although those trips occur often to see family, I never installed a TV screen in our car either. On long-distance trips, we talk, we play games such as "I Spy with My Little Eye," we invent car games, we have sat in boredom, we have gotten back to some more games, discussions, etc. But we have not used a digital device to entertain our daughter, so she doesn't feel bored on a long-distance drive or a rare restaurant visit. The few times we have taken our daughter to a restaurant, she liked to walk around until the food came, which we did.

My husband and I would walk around the restaurant with her. She liked to say hi to people at neighboring tables. Otherwise, we just talked. I understand there is an educational component to using digital devices, and some content can be beneficial. But I see it too often when even toddlers are exposed to excessive screen time, and I am convinced no matter how 'educational' the content that keeps them glued to the digital device is, it hinders their development of other essential skills, such as cognitive development. More and more children don't seem like they can carry on a moderately meaningful conversation. I have been engaging my child in discussions since day one. When she was a baby, I would tell her how blessed I felt to have her, how wonderful she was, how excited I was to watch her grow, and what things we'd do and places we'd see. At one point, I even apologized to her in advance for all the mistakes I would probably make and that each one would come from a place of love for her, and most of them would probably be safety-related. As a week- or months-old baby, she had not the slightest idea of what I was saying, but she was getting used to my voice and used to communicate. Now, she knows how to initiate a discussion and converse with adults and children for extended periods. How's that for navigating boredom? There are a few things more meaningful than face-to-face, heart-to-heart conversations.

I find it far more beneficial to think of boredom as the trigger leading to desired or undesired outcomes. An undesired outcome would be your child's whining, crying, upset, or downright angry when in boredom, leading to the child getting what they want, and what they want is something related to instant gratification and a temporary fix. One of the primary emotions associated with boredom is frustration. The feeling of being stuck in a monotonous routine or engaging in non-stimulating activities can lead to a sense of irritation and restlessness. It feels as if time slows down, and the mind craves novelty and excitement. A desired outcome would be the behavior you would like to help your child build when bored—a behavior your child will benefit from not just at the moment but long-term. This is a game-changer. Working with my child from this perspective and in this way, I redirect the trigger (in this case, boredom) toward a desired outcome.

I frame boredom as a cue to instigate a specific action to achieve a desired result. So many books are written on habits and how to build and maintain them. These books have nothing to do with boredom or parenting. Still, they can be beneficial if you are interested in reframing your reaction to your child's boredom or your perceived notion of boredom through building habits that can be instrumental in your personal growth and as a parent. I also use this book genre to help my child build habits. Not all boredom is equal. One thing I do when my child experiences boredom is to ask myself, how is my child articulating to me that she is bored? What's the way she presents the fact that she is bored? What's her physical stance? What's her facial expression? These are very small yet crucial clues for me as a parent to be able to see right through my child. This is not meant in an accusatory way by any stretch of the imagination! It is also not meant to be a set-up for a "got you" moment. It is genuinely intended to practice knowing my child on a deep level so that when boredom arises, I can respond in a meaningful, helpful, and caring way!

Suppose my child's primary emotion is sadness as she tells me she's bored. In that case, that's my cue to pretty much bump up her immediate need to the top of my priority list because this emotional facet is rooted in the perceived lack of fulfillment or purpose. This kind of boredom needs more than sitting with it. It requires a conversation because unaddressed sadness can lead to subtle melancholy setting in. If I brushed off this sadness and told her she could use an electronic device or play in her room to entertain herself, I would inadvertently push her into muddy waters. She gets no benefit from that. Also, the last thing I want to do if my child is displaying sad boredom is to direct her to something that feels like a reward. Why? When done enough times, it sends a message and builds a type of habit that suggests feeling sad equals being rewarded. So, no, thank you. With my child, this would be the time I would do a stop-and-drop because this is the time she may need something more than just a creative outlet. There may be what I, figuratively speaking, like to call underlying "running waters" that must be navigated before a tsunami hits.

Besides sadness, another emotional expression of boredom I am looking for is isolation because this potentially leads to feelings of loneliness, which leads to sadness and a perceived lack of fulfillment or purpose. So, as you can see, it's a vicious cycle. These readily available emotions are open for grabs, and children can discover them quicker than you can say 'fun' (pun intended). None of these emotions are fun, and experienced briefly may even be healthy (an enormous asterisk by the word healthy); however, unaddressed, these seemingly non-threatening emotional experiences can lead to the development of seemingly out-of-nowhere big and not-so-healthy running waters. For these reasons, I see childhood boredom as the ultimate opportunity to create space for children to build their emotional awareness as early as possible. Of course, every child is different, but this is where the mother/caregiver plays a significant role in connecting and strengthening that parent-child bond! For some parents, this can be a challenge. There is nothing wrong with acknowledging that and asking for help from peers and professionals. Our personalities, circumstances, and life are quite different. So, we must collectively become better than judge each other because if we are willing to judge, we must also be willing to go a step deeper and offer to help. If we believe we know how to do it better, we need to do it better by reflecting and acting. Again, this is where we need to put real effort into building better communities where we help each other in meaningful ways and lift each other in how we show up for our children first and for other parents second.

I encourage boredom with my child because that helps her to get to know herself better. When she's bored and, because of her boredom, she thinks of something to do, like creating a project, reading a book, or coming up with an idea she feels proud of, I know she grew an inch taller in mental and emotional awareness. By one inch, she is emotionally more intelligent than she was when she started. Of course, just because she handles boredom like a pro once doesn't mean she has completely mastered the martial art that is boredom. It takes practice and repetition; that takes time, patience, and a lot of guidance from, you guessed it, the mother or primary caregiver. And that is what we must focus on as a society and a culture. The intention is for my child to understand that feeling bored is not something she needs to avoid or run from; it's something to learn how to use to her advantage; it's an opportunity, not a blocker. I have been using boredom with my daughter as a catalyst for creativity for years. It has worked well. Why? Because when the mind is not occupied with external stimuli, it opens to creative thoughts and ideas. This positive aspect of boredom highlights its potential as a creative force, showcasing that moments of idleness can spark innovative thinking and a problem-solving attitude. The biggest threat to using boredom as a positive tool in a child's development is the level of attachment parents have to social media and the internet. While most consider living in the digital age to be convenient, liberating, exciting, and novel, living in this age has introduced a new dimension to boredom—the fear of missing out (FOMO), which can exacerbate feelings of boredom. Paradoxically, the overwhelming online options can leave individuals feeling unfulfilled, as the constant pursuit of the next stimulating activity becomes a source of dissatisfaction. Think about it; if it's hard for adults to avoid this phenomenon, how can children? After all, children model the adults in their lives.

6

Boredom In A Hyperconnected World

Helping Children Move Beyond Constant Stimulation

I talk about boredom a lot because when I look around, I see people, regardless of age, constantly fighting boredom. This affects our children and how they view and respond to boredom and, by extension, how they respond to other aspects of life. For example, the simple act of waiting in line is no longer considered socially 'normal.' Without giving it any thought, people reach for their digital device (usually a cell phone) and start aimlessly scrolling to fill in the waiting time so they are not bored. Watching your child during an extracurricular activity like ballet or gymnastics as a simple act is not enough – you must do something not to feel bored. Connecting with another person sitting next to you through a conversation is no longer viewed as socially 'normal' either – you must pull out a cell phone and look occupied so you are not bored or, God forbid, engaged in a boring conversation. Observing many of these kinds of instances all around me drove me to make a promise to myself while I was waiting and hoping to experience motherhood.

When I finally got pregnant and had my child, I told myself I would do everything in my power to be fully present for my child. I'm not going to say it's easy because trying to operate analog in a digital world is not easy, and, let's face it, it's a bit off-putting – going against the grain is not easy. But I will say it is worth celebrating. I will also note with patience, practice, and mindfulness, it becomes easier. Yes, it requires what appears to be a 24-7 on-my-toes attitude toward a promise I have made to myself, and it can be pretty exhausting for people around me to watch. I get that. I don't prioritize thinking about that. I'm baffled by the fact that, on a conversation level, most people will agree we know all this. But only maybe half of those people agree with it in theory, and the other half have a completely different view on life and parenting, so they find this to be unnecessary, even nonsensical. But the truth is, very few agree with this execution. I will be the first one to say I have times when I have failed in delivering my promise because, you guessed it, it's hard! But hard isn't where effort stops; it's where it begins! I have successfully executed my promise about 90% of the time. For the rest of my time, I am open to improvement.

In the context of our current cultural and societal landscape, being in a state of boredom is most often perceived as a deviation from the expectations and responsibilities ingrained in our daily lives. In a world that values productivity, constant connectivity, and achievement, boredom can be seen as a counterforce that challenges these norms. This transfers to our children. This is why we must become and remain aware of the tension between our well-being and the external pressure we tend to succumb to, especially if we want to show up for our children in a meaningful and sustainable way as they grow up.

One fundamental aspect to consider is the emphasis on productivity. I have personally struggled with productivity for a long time. Even now, I must consciously remind myself to be hyper-alert about how I go about productivity and that it doesn't distract me from the things that matter more in life. I do this because I can easily fall into a trap I create for myself when I team up with my "bestie" Perfection and chase after productivity. That's a recipe for getting stuck. Although modern societies celebrate a culture of constant busyness and productivity, often equating one's worth with one's activity level, we can't point the finger at someone or something and leave it at that. For example, we can't just blame social media for how things are and continue going about our day. That's not even half the battle – it's simply an easy way out of our responsibility and accountability toward ourselves and our community. Suppose we are willing to recognize that there is a problem on social and cultural levels with social media. In that case, we also need to have the guts to ask what I can do on a personal, family, and social level to correct this problem.

Then start doing it—however small the attempt. We must start somewhere. And when we fail, because we will fail multiple times, go back and do it again! Fail differently. In the process of all our failures, individually and as a group, a solution will be born to benefit all of us. But most people don't do this. Most people don't stick with what they say beyond making a point in a conversation. And those who do are not doing it loud enough. Why? Because, by comparison, they are few and far between. Because it's hard! Because for many, when the going gets hard, it's easier to look for solace in belonging to whatever the latest trend is put before us. Unfortunately, what's portrayed is a lack of willingness to go as far as it takes. What's depicted is that our belief in the cause is weak. It is easier to scroll through social media and laugh at a funny video someone posted of themselves or, worse, their child to briefly escape reality using entertainment for both the entertainer and the entertained. Sure, it puts the person in a temporary state of good mood to see the likes and comments supporting the funny video. But what does it do long-term, and what does it do to the child being filmed when they are fed entertaining lines to say or being asked tailoring questions leading to responses that indeed add to the number of likes for that video but undermine the negative effect on children in the long run? In the meantime, although you have already temporarily dodged the feeling of being overwhelmed, you have just fallen deeper into wiring your brain to believe that you can't change the world, so why try?

The notion that every moment must be filled with purposeful endeavors can get quite exhausting, but in a society that glorifies the "hustle" and the pursuit of success as a measure of happiness, moments of idleness are viewed as unproductive and not good enough. This notion can negatively impact children into adulthood, especially regarding their self-image, conduct, and relationship with productivity. I will argue that information overload can also lead to boredom. It's hard to fight against something so massive as the digital age we live in. It has contributed to an environment where constant stimulation is the norm. Social media, streaming services, and many online activities provide endless options to fill our time. But the mere existence of social media and technological progress in our humanity isn't the problem.

We make it a problem. We, humans, make it a problem in how we use it, so I avoid blaming social media, technology, or electronics for our social and cultural issues; I blame us, the people. I stand by it when I say that we have proved irresponsible and unfit to navigate our way through technological progress so far. Sure, there is a component of over-generalization here, I get that, but there is a fundamental truth that we need to wake up to and accept and get to work to make it better!! For our children's sake. The truth is that the more we are in the world of technology, the more idle we become and the more distant from each other. We need to stop pretending things are fine the way they are. Because they are not. There is acceptance and encouragement, and then there is crossing the line. However, as is the case with most things, there are limits and reasons for those limits. There is a point where the level of accepting and encouraging everything for the sake of being encouraging and fearlessly crossing the line eventually leads to what may look like a harmless ditch but is, in fact, an abyss from which there is no point of return. That's where we are headed with the way we use technological progress. This affects all of us, but our children and their children will have to experience the consequences or the rewards of our actions. It's up to us, and we need help as the list of potential implications keeps growing. Let's change that!

Often, I talk to my child about fully understanding the rules before breaking them. Listen to understand other perspectives before dismissing them. But I also talk a lot about not going along for the sake of belonging. When I have these kinds of discussions with her, I have them in a way that raises her awareness of feelings of boredom, to recognize them, and to know what to do. Because if there is sadness in the kind of boredom she experiences, I want her to be able to recognize that and do a quick and honest inventory of her world. If she experiences going along for the sake of belonging in any area of her world, but the belonging doesn't feel right, I want her to sit in that boredom enough to face it and then get out and do something about it. One thing

I like to do with my daughter when she comes to me with "I'm bored" is a dialogue that would read something like this:

My daughter: *I'm bored.*

Me: *...And?*

My daughter: *And I want to do something, but I don't know what that is.*

Me: *I'm not sure what that is either. Maybe I can help, but who do you think can best figure this out?*

My daughter (wide smile on her face): *Probably me.*

Me (returning the same wide smile): *Where would you start?* Her brain is already engaged, and I can see her creativity sparkle in her eyes.

My daughter: *I know. How about I make a list of all the things I like to do, and then I put numbers next to each thing in order from my favorite to my least favorite, and then maybe I keep that list...* This goes on for another ten minutes, perhaps until she goes through the whole process she planned out, getting increasingly excited as she keeps coming up with more options. I didn't provide a solution by telling her what to play with or giving her a tablet to watch something. I asked her simple questions and waited.

Another "I'm bored" dialogue would read something like this:

My daughter: *I'm bored.*

Me: *...And?*

My daughter: *And I want to do something, but I want to do it with you, but you are working.*

(I work from home, so although I consider it a blessing, it can be challenging in situations like the one above. As much as my daughter understands that while I work, she needs to be patient and wait until I'm done, she is a child, and this concept doesn't always sit well.)

Me: *There is nothing I would rather do than play with you. I am working right now, but that doesn't mean I am choosing work over you. It means that at this moment, I need to take care of work first so I can play with you later without disruptions.*

My daughter: *I know, mama...*

Me: *Can we think of something for you to do in the meantime?*

There we go. Again, I can see those gears turning through the sparks in her eyes.

My daughter: *I got it! How about we do a science project, and I set up the lab? If I'm done setting up the lab before you are done with work while I'm waiting, I can...*

This is how I handle boredom with my child, and it works every time. I understand this approach may not work for every child, but it's an excellent point to start and experiment with through trial and error. Another thing I do is later in the day; I make sure I bring up the instance of boredom and compliment her on how she handled it. I don't compliment her outcome, but the effort she put into working toward the outcome (doing the activity of her choice). Getting to this kind of dialogue is also not an isolated approach. It's part of a chain that started from the day she came into this world, from the day I brought her home with me as the most amazing bundle of joy God has blessed me and my husband with! Small, seemingly insignificant parenting choices pay dividends when you stack them up over time. I genuinely believe that. Boredom is not a child's nemesis. Boredom provides opportunities for children to take a little time and space with themselves so they can do what I call reflective discovery. Reflective discovery is when my child reflects on what she likes to do, what she doesn't want to do, the games and toys she prefers to play with, and the friends she has similarities with. Through reflective discovery, I am simply guiding her to run an inventory in her mind and, by doing so, discover something about herself along the way. It's pretty interesting to observe.

A constant state of connectivity is yet another concept that needs monitoring regarding boredom. The prevalence of smartphones and the internet being available to young children creates an environment where they expect to be constantly entertained; if not, they start to feel their nemesis: boredom. Boredom is not necessarily a sign of laziness or disinterest; instead, it can signal that moments of recharge and reflection are needed. I find it especially beneficial for my child to understand this. Embracing boredom as a natural part of the human experience early on can lead to a more balanced and sustainable approach to life. A life not filled with stuff and entertainment as distractions. A life filled with meaning. It doesn't help that our society lacks the tools and techniques to address children's emotional state of boredom. Although there is a growing awareness of the importance of emotional well-being in children, the focus revolves around some more significant and apparent challenges that have already manifested and need to be mended and managed rather than prevented. In other words, the focus is and continues to be on treating rather than preventing boredom, which continues to be viewed as something to be eliminated as quickly as possible. To shift to better ways of addressing boredom, there are a few things we need to be conscious of and have an actual open discussion about.

First, acknowledge that children, like adults, experience boredom but may lack the vocabulary and understanding to express it constructively. Unlike visible emotions such as joy or sadness, boredom can be elusive and challenging to articulate.

Second, we demand that our educational system, a central aspect of a child's life, address boredom effectively because that is not the case currently. For example, giving children pop-it gadgets or squishes or whatever else to use in class during moments they 'feel bored' reinforces the idea that if you are bored, you need to do something so you don't feel bored and potentially disruptive. I firmly believe we need educators with the tools to recognize boredom in children and use that to foster an environment that encourages curiosity and participation in learning how to sit in boredom instead of how to remedy boredom. We need educators who can work with children to help them understand how to navigate through boredom, how to use boredom to invite creativity and learn about themselves, and how to be and grow as individuals while feeling bored at times. How do we expect children to find themselves as adults without giving them the time, the space, and the tools needed to learn about themselves? There is a whole lot that a person can learn about themselves through boredom. That starts by connecting with other human beings and not objects and fidgets. We must create opportunities to connect on a human-to-human level, not jump to the next available electronic device or fidgeting object.

Third, limit technology in our children's lives. Digital devices are viewed as a go-to for remedying boredom. The excuse is that we are so busy and stretched thin these days as adults that sometimes it's just necessary to calm a child down for a "few" minutes by giving them a digital device – putting a screen in front of them to stare at. The socially accepted response seems to be "just until I collect my sanity back." How about making a child run circles around the house instead of staring at a digital screen? Because while the adult is collecting their sanity, the digital device is infiltrating the child's brain and claiming a significant role in that child's behavior. The moment a digital device is chosen as a method and a tool to calm down an irritated child, that very moment the parent signs up to become part of the vicious cycle of using external entertainment as a companion for the child in more and more instances. The child learns that displaying irritation can get them what they want and that a moment of simply being is a condition to be remedied. The remedy is screen-based entertainment – time mentally and emotionally away from family and friends. While these digital devices can often contain educational content alongside entertainment, excessive screen time contributes to the emotional state usually labeled as boredom when it is indeed a state of overload. Overload to the point where the brain needs a change in the form of a break. But children don't know how to articulate brain overload, so they say they are bored as in bored being something to be rescued from immediately when, in fact, boredom should do the opposite and give children time to reflect on what they sponged in from the digital device before moving onto the next best distraction without processing what they just absorbed. I like to take these breaks with my daughter when it comes to any content consumption.

I facilitate a safe space for her to process what she consumes and decide if and how that may fit within our family beliefs and principles. Through discussion, we determine if it's value-in or garbage-out. I don't just put her in front of the TV or any electronic device and walk away to do my grownup stuff. I sit with her. I watch with her. I watch her reactions as she watches. It's a lot. I know. Is it necessary? You decide for your child. As for me and my child, it is essential and fun!

There is so much content online, and unfortunately, most of it is garbage because, as I said earlier, we humans are not intelligent and responsible about how we apply technology in our lives. There are no guardrails as to what adds value and can hold space for consumption and what's just noise and shouldn't take space—nope, anything goes!

Back to our children: For a child to know how to navigate the emotional state of boredom, someone would need to work with that child from discovering boredom to understanding boredom as a good thing, to sitting with boredom, to navigating what happens during boredom, all the way through growing out of boredom. In other words, a child must be guided and coached to work with boredom, not run away from it.

The fourth and final is parental involvement. This is crucial in addressing a child's emotional state, including boredom. However, parents are unprepared to navigate the nuanced landscape of their children's boredom. This is a societal challenge, and we all need to start stepping up and getting involved in it. We need to step away from 'I' and 'me' in parenting, such as the overemphasized and, quite honestly, overrated "me-time" as a parent. Yes, of course, we all need to step out of all our roles at times, but I'm observing a lot more misuse and overuse of such "me-time" moments and a lot less of an actual meaningful, helpful way of being a parent. Perhaps, as a society, if we build better support systems around parenting and hold space for each other in an open, honest, educational, and guiding way, parents would not long for or feel the need for "me-time" nearly as much as I currently see and hear from parents. Again, I'm not disputing that you may need time for yourself as a parent occasionally. However, we are very much an individualistic society that has been and continues to condition us into needs for the self (self-realization, self-care, self-improvement, etc.), keeping us separate rather than connected and coming together, really together, to help each other as parents and as individual members of a group without judging, without personal agendas. Just for the sake of lifting each other and our children up. Our consumer-driven culture often bombards children with a constant stream of entertainment options. While this may seem like fun and a solution to boredom on the surface, it can contribute to a cycle of instant gratification, overstimulation, and entitlement. Preventing this needs to be our number one priority as parents. Parents who build and maintain small parent communities and raise our children such that they have a center to return to so they don't find themselves lost and lonely. Teaching our children the value of patience, delayed gratification, and the joy of creating their entertainment far from digital devices can be powerful in cultivating emotional resilience. It can also equip our children to know how to navigate technology rather than be navigated by technology as we are headed toward the Age of AI.

Additionally, boredom can be linked to practicing mindfulness with children, which is a valuable way of navigating the emotional state of boredom. Again, children need to be introduced to and guided into this concept so they understand its importance and how to use it. Mindfulness encourages children to be present in the moment, fostering an awareness of their thoughts and feelings. As parents, when we teach our children techniques such as deep breathing and meditation exercises, we provide them with practical tools to navigate moments of boredom and develop emotional regulation skills to serve them for a lifetime.

7

Always Start with the Truth

Shifting Focus from Materialism to Relationships

My child was introduced to Santa as a fictional character derived from a legend. There are varying versions of the legend, but, in a nutshell, it's about a person who lived in luxury and extravagance, decided to give all of it up, and used his wealth to deliver gifts to children as far and wide as he could go, especially to those whose parents weren't able to provide beyond what was necessary for survival. That person from the legend came to be known as St. Nicholas, and somehow, in this culture, he became associated with Christmas—thank you, consumerism. My family celebrates Christian Orthodox Christmas (January 7) and Christian Catholic Christmas (December 25). In our household, Christmas is celebrated as the birth of Christ. That's it. In our household, a fictional character doesn't cross over into this reality, doesn't invade our privacy through the chimney, or buy gifts using our bank account.

Celebrating Christmas according to the old calendar (January 7) and the new calendar (December 25) has been helpful because it has allowed my family to separate honoring the birth of Christ from honoring Santa and his presents. It seems like Christmas (as celebrated in our society) is a bit conflicting. If you are a Christian believer, this can confuse a child, especially a highly curious one. For example, if Christmas is when Christ was born, what does Santa have to do with the birth of Jesus Christ? Was he there when Christ was born? I am posing these questions because my child asked these very questions. So, for December 25th, my daughter and I prepare cookies, milk, and a couple of presents from Mommy and Daddy under the Christmas tree, and one handmade present each of us makes and puts in the stockings. We get up in the morning, have our cookies and milk (coffee for me and my husband) while she opens our presents to her, and we spend the rest of the day playing board games, watching some TV, and just enjoying being together. Last year, we watched the musical that came out about the birth of Christ, and the year before, we watched a couple of animated short movies and series made for kids about the birth of Christ. Then, on January 7th, we celebrate the birth of Christ. We go to church, then meet at my parents' house for dinner. We spend the day together as a family, including Bible stories for the kids to hear, ask questions, and have family-friendly discussions.

As a child growing up in Eastern Europe, nobody had to tell me at age 12 that Santa wasn't real. I pretty much knew from the get-go. So did all my friends. So did everyone! Having lived in the United States for most of my adult life, it is fascinating to me, as a society, how far we are willing to go and stay united in keeping something so trivial as a lie alive, yet we are so unwilling to collaborate on fronts that make a difference in people's lives, like building and maintaining parenting communities, taking care of people experiencing homelessness, properly and rapidly addressing climate change, or, hey, how about reforming our education system? How much energy we put into nurturing and forcing this lie onto our children is mind-blowing, yet how uninterested and withdrawn we are about most real problems we are dealing with as humanity.

It is my prerogative that, regardless of popular belief, raising a child with the understanding that Santa Claus is not real can have various benefits, contributing to their cognitive, emotional, and social development. Yes, the tradition of Santa can be 'magical' for many families. Yes, it can be harder to opt for transparency, although I will argue the 'hard' part is self-inflicted in this society. Namely, it's hard because someone at some point decided to spread joy based on a lie (how fitting, lol), and it became so big, and so much time has passed that people don't question it; they go along with it. But opting for transparency about the origin of the Santa story and the gifts he supposedly flies across the world and delivers in one night can foster critical thinking, empathy, and a deeper connection with reality. Below are the arguments I would like to make point-by-point about why I decided to raise my child with the truth about Santa. Also, at the end of each point, where applicable, I will add my experience with my child.

Critical thinking skills. I believe when children are encouraged to question the existence of Santa, they engage in a process of logical thinking that leads to reasoning. Reasoning early on helps them analyze information, consider evidence, and arrive at conclusions based on rational thinking. Of course, they don't realize it in big words like these, but that's why they have us, their parent(s), to provide this context and guide them. It lays the foundation for a mindset that will be valuable throughout their lives, from academics to problem-solving in real-world scenarios. How do they apply "magic" in the real world? Telling my child the truth about the hype around Santa was right, and I have not regretted it. One thing I could have done better, in retrospect, is instead of introducing Santa as a fictional character from the beginning, I could have created the space for my child to practice her natural inclination toward curiosity so she would have arrived at the truth throughout a few discussions—same outcome, but perhaps better facilitation. In retrospect, that would have required going along with the Santa story for a little bit, which I didn't want to do. Also, in retrospect, I don't think this would have worked out well with my child, who, at age two and a half, after watching a Mickey Mouse Christmas episode, asked how Santa would fit in the chimney we don't have, does that mean he wouldn't come to our house, and why wouldn't he just come through the front door. Hmm.... :) Always start with the truth.

Trust. I believe trust is a fundamental element in any relationship, especially in the relationships we build with children. Being truthful with my child about Santa reinforced the credibility of our parental guidance, and it has extended to other areas of life, fostering open communication and a sense of security in our daughter. The argument stands that other things in raising children contribute to the trust factor in the parent-child relationship. I wholeheartedly agree. However, I also believe the age-old concept that trust is built over a long period, yet it takes one act, one time, one lie to make trust vanish, while it takes a lifetime and, in some cases, it's close to impossible to rebuild trust once lost entirely. I firmly believe trust is ongoing. Trust is one of those things that, once broken, leaves a mark.

Sure, things can always be mended, and many 'things' (like Santa) can be explained and justified. But that feeling of being lied to tends to remain and linger. I chose to change that for my child. I recognize many people who read this will disagree. That's ok. I can't go along to belong. We'd have to agree to disagree and find a different topic to connect over. Telling my child the truth, even at times I felt it might temporarily make things worse, has made parenting more complex and liberating at the same time. I wouldn't have it any other way. I want to note here that there have been times when telling the truth is not age-appropriate. Instead of telling a "safe lie" or a half-truth, I have told her we must leave the topic open until she can comprehend the truth. This can be very difficult for a curious child such as my daughter, but it works if done consistently and with mindfulness.

Empathy. Introducing Santa as a fictional figure can help children learn that not every child receives the same level of gifts directly tied to their behavior throughout the year, as 'Santa' claims. There are many children out there whose parents didn't or couldn't strike a deal with Santa despite their children being well-behaved (maybe even better-behaved than most kids who got what they wished for from Santa) year-round. Although we don't want to inundate children with information on financial challenges and struggles to scare them, they do need to know and be guided to understand how to appreciate and value material possessions. Children these days lack that appreciation. Children need to be taught the value of not getting everything they want. It's okay not to have the newest gadget or a particular gadget at all. Discussions about economic disparities and empathy towards those who may be less fortunate are of immense importance in raising our children into well-rounded individuals with a realistic and thoughtful outlook on life. Instead of attributing disparities to a mythical figure's judgment, children can learn that the joy of giving is rooted in compassion and understanding of others. Spending time with someone is a far greater gift than anything money can buy.

I did two things with my child when she was a toddler. First, whenever possible, I avoided taking her shopping with me. This minimized and eliminated exposure to the world of consumerism around her. I have my parents to be eternally grateful for always being available to watch my daughter whenever I needed to go to the store. My mom retired when my brother and sister-in-law had their child six months before my daughter was born. Second, when I did take my daughter to a store with me (when she was a little older), I would explain before walking into the store something like this trip does not include buying a toy, or something like on this trip, we can get one toy. I made sure I mixed toy and non-toy trips, but I made sure the toy trips were far less than the non-toy trips. During toy trips, she was guided to pick only one toy. Not two small ones in place of one big one. No. It was always one. I did my best to guide her to decide based on what she liked and what she would use/play with more rather than what was flashier or bigger. It worked. She caught on to this concept quickly. Maybe I was just lucky due to her personality, or perhaps it was because I just gave it a go and stayed consistent, or both. It worked. Even today, at eight years old, she still goes for what she feels she has a use for rather than buy as a result of instant gratification kicking in. Recently, we talked about how she needs two more pairs of jeans. I went online, and we found the ones she liked. We go through styles together and narrow things down, but she makes the final decision. I put the pairs she wanted in the cart and suggested another cute pair. This was the dialogue we had:

Me: *Look at this pair. It'll look so cute on you! Do you like it?*
My daughter: *Oh yeah! That's cute! But we already got the two pairs I love. I only need two.*
Me: *That's ok, you'll have one extra.*
My daughter: *No, I'm good.*

I wanted to get that pair for her, but I appreciated her modesty and respected her decision. Was one pair of jeans a big deal? No, not at all. But it was one small decision in millions of decisions she has made and will continue to make that will shape who she becomes. And I am happy she knows modesty and practices making decisions confidently rather than confusing her by getting an extra pair of jeans just because I think they will look cute.

Inclusive environment. Many year-round holidays have become the centerpiece of our children's school curriculum. This has contributed to most families with diverse religious backgrounds, who may not celebrate Christmas and who may have different traditions, being pushed to celebrate Santa's holiday due to unspoken, subtle (or not so subtle) peer pressure coming directly from school. As I mentioned before, my family is Christian Orthodox. We celebrate Christmas, but the pressure to do Santa stuff doesn't come from family and friends (they already know me and know my stance); it comes from my child's classroom. My daughter has asked me if Santa was real, would he "drop off" presents to houses where Christmas is not celebrated, or would he skip them? Yeah, this is what my daughter asked me. And then she followed it with: "Good thing I know Santa's not real because that would be confusing!" I said, yeah, it would be for both Santa and us. Then we both burst into a laugh… I love these little moments with my daughter! I call them "moments of child wisdom" that I get to absorb.

Schools need to exclude or at least tone it down with activities emphasizing events that should stay outside the classroom. Sure, there can be a mention of upcoming holidays and celebratory expressions exchanged. Still, we are taking it too far, especially with Christmas presents and Halloween costumes. By acknowledging cultural diversity in celebrations, children learn to respect and appreciate different perspectives, promoting inclusivity and understanding in our multicultural society. We like to claim this inclusivity but fall short of practicing it. Let's take, for example, classroom parties that schools have around the holidays where each parent is to send their child to school with some trinkets for the entire class. The class exchanges those trinkets with each other for short-lived excitement. Once children go home, those trinkets lose their value and are most often forgotten. And we rinse and repeat this every holiday, year after year, while slowly and subliminally engraving consumerism in our children's minds. We mark each holiday with stuff. Instead, why not invest time and effort in bringing children together in the classroom through sharing holiday stories and asking each other questions about how each kid celebrates the specific holiday at home with family and friends? Or why not bring each class closer together by organizing holiday gatherings open to parents, students, and teacher(s)? Maybe schedule these gatherings on different days for different classes. Perhaps we make each gathering about the conversation, about parents connecting to other parents, about children observing this connection among adults and modeling a similar kind of vibe among each other. Make it about each teacher, parent, and student learning and experiencing the Spirit of the Holidays through stories, laughter, support, and even tears if that's what's needed. Make it about building relationships that bring communities together. We don't do that. We buy stuff to compensate for a good conversation. That's not meaningful; it's superficial and needs to change.

Cause and effect. All I have to say is that when children are taught that gifts result from someone's effort (and not some magical figure), whether their parents, relatives, or friends, it instills a sense of responsibility and reciprocity. Reducing the materialistic focus often associated with the holiday season allows children to appreciate the thought and effort of selecting and giving gifts. This shift in perspective fosters gratitude and a deeper understanding of the value of relationships over material possessions.

One way I captured this in my parenting was by putting my daughter's natural inclination toward art to work by encouraging her to make birthday and holiday cards or to draw something of her choosing on an existing card. She loved this a lot, especially during ages 3-6. Another way I captured the cause and effect when it came to the materialistic focus associated with the holiday season is by explaining to my daughter where presents come from. My daughter knows her presents for any occasion come from her parents or other people, not magic. She also knows that people must work to earn money to spend money and that in spending money, we make choices based on need and purpose, not on temporary excitement. You may think this is a load for a child to carry around. I beg to differ. It's a tool to keep her on the right side of expectations when she comes in direct contact with adulthood.

8
A Call For Change

Building Parenting Communities and Policies

I stayed home with my child for the first three and a half years of her life. Every day, I am grateful I was able to do that. I have been working from home for the following four and a half years of her life. Every day, I am equally grateful for that. If it is not clear yet, I would like to reiterate that I firmly believe that if a woman is blessed with the gift of becoming a mother, she needs to stay home with her child. She needs to act as the child's primary caregiver for at least the first two years following the birth of her child—some countries, such as Sweden, built on this parenting model following years of confirming research. Staying home beyond the first two years is a bonus. I want to make one thing clear: I'm not talking about staying home while you have babysitters or grandparents watch your children. While these roles play an essential part, I am only focusing on staying home as the primary caregiver for the child. I'm talking about actual, active staying home with your child, as in talking, playing, and laughing with your child; as in tucking them in bed every night; as in waking up every hour of the night when they can't sleep or are sick or just scared; as in staying with them all night if that's what they need during those first two years and beyond, depending on your child. That's the kind of staying-at-home I'm talking about. I have been and will continue to be, criticized for this, but I will say it anyway: the moment I decided to become a mother, I decided to put my needs and comfort secondary. There. I said it. Again. For those making frowning faces right now, you can still have your life and your 'me-time,' and I'm not saying that's unimportant. But I am saying it is no longer as important. Until, of course, you become an empty nester (a term I despise from the bottom of my heart, but that's a topic for another time). As parents, we go through waves and must make tough choices. I have. But through it all, knowing and understanding your why is crucial! It's vital to understand who you are as a person. Understand that you can't and should not feel you must pursue everything! At once!

There is this push for us women to allow society to inflict on us that if we can do it all, we are worthy, and only then can we be accepted as contributing members of our small, local, and larger communities. We push it onto ourselves as well. We can get competitive and mean to each other for no reason other than to prove ourselves to society. For example, the "girl power" movement often feels off-putting. It's not the movement's goals that I find distasteful, but rather the approach. We don't need catchy slogans and consumer products to validate our relevance. Real change requires hard work and dedication. This principle also applies to parenting; children especially need the presence and care of their mothers or primary caregivers. This needs to be one person. One person needs to be in the role of what I like to call parenting ownership. It's part of AgileParenting™. It would be best if you had someone with the final say. Children need this. Children must be raised by their parents in presence, not in theory. For that to happen, we need to pivot on a cultural and societal level because, unfortunately, as it currently stands, our system for supporting parents is broken. Awareness efforts are not loud enough, strong enough, pushy enough! We need to consider this for the sake of our children. We need to start experimenting with changing our system, and we need to start with education. We must begin making bolder actions, let ourselves fail, and then try something else. When we fail at that, we must keep trying and looking for different ways to fail until we find what works best. But awareness, theory, and consideration are last season's acts. We need to roll up our sleeves and get to work.

Women and men. Together. Now. For the sake of our children. Not every parent has been as fortunate as I have been to stay home with their child without worrying about how they will provide necessities for their children if they don't go to work. A woman works as a mother for the first two years of her child's life to bond and set the foundation for her child's proper development. Supporting women in doing this is the most significant investment this country can make. Invest in mothers who want to stay home with their children and help them when ready to return to work without penalizing them for the time gap they were not part of the workforce. We must start investing in proper parenting, starting with mothers as primary caregivers. This topic requires discussions that go beyond the scope of this book but are incredibly relevant. For example, changes in policies need to be made that include compensating mothers for the duration of their parenting sabbatical (at least one but optimally two years from the birth of a child), guaranteed job placement upon the end of the parenting sabbatical, as well as total health benefits for at least the child/children during that period. So much can be done if we only begin to change our mindset and the policies around quality in the work-life balance arena.

Equally crucial is to start investing in our education system. Our education system is conflicted in meeting the evolving needs of children today. One critical aspect is the shift from a traditional, one-size-fits-all approach to a more personalized and flexible model that fosters critical thinking, creativity, and adaptability. Yes, there are programs and modules instilled in some schools depending on the school district, but these programs' level of application and success varies. As a parent, I feel like there is a lot of noise around new programs schools are trying to implement that fall short in their application because new concepts are being forced into existing processes. That inflates current issues and makes things more complicated instead of simplified. This needs to change, and there are a few things that I'm sure we already know that need to change, but I will list them anyway.

Applicability. The current system often emphasizes and tests children's ability to recall facts rather than their capacity to apply knowledge. This approach does not adequately prepare them for real-world challenges, where problem-solving and creative thinking are essential. A reformed education system should prioritize coaching rather than teaching methods that cultivate collaboration and a deep understanding of concepts and encourage analytical thinking. Methods that allow space for each child to learn horizontally by ways of associating and connecting concepts while developing their baseline, not vertically by piling up knowledge to memorize long enough to pass a test but not be able to retain and make practical use of it when called for. We need to stop grading students based on points for successful short-term memorization of information and start grading them on their effort in developing and following their process and the lessons they learn from the outcomes they produced based on their process. For this kind of transformation to occur, we need to reexamine how future educators are being prepared for their roles in the classroom. The role of teachers must evolve and be redefined. Teaching should no longer be solely about the academic and social transfer of knowledge through checklists and performance reviews aimed at collecting points. It must extend beyond its traditional definition to encompass skills such as coaching, relationship building, collaboration, teamwork, and community building. The most effective way to achieve this is by developing programs where the acquisition and application of knowledge happen concurrently rather than as separate, time-bound events. In other words, theory and practice should be integrated and co-occur. This shift must begin within the classroom, viewing the teacher as a learner.

The rapid pace of technological advancements requires an educational framework that integrates digital literacy in appropriate intervals and prevents creating dependency on these devices. Yes, we need to be in lockstep with technological advancement, but we also need to teach our children how to use technology, not how to be used by it. Incorporating coding, digital skills, and an understanding of emerging technologies provides children with the foundation to navigate the digital landscape in their future careers. However, undermining their social and emotional connections to other human beings may rob them of the very careers they will be after. Most careers require human interaction at one point or another. Building relationships with other human beings is one of the most important aspects of any job. There must be a balance. Currently, if there is such a balance claimed, it is superficial. As a parent, I do not see any benefit to my child using electronics from an early age, especially in the K-4 classroom. These formative years are best spent connected to nature and learning through outdoor activities at home and school. Children need guidance during these years with activities and tasks that facilitate working together, helping and learning from each other, respecting each other and their elderly, and building meaningful relationships. They need not be graded or tested for academic performance and placement during these early years. Instead, they need human connection, not virtual reality. Teachers can use technology for their work and time management, but there is no need for students in early education to use electronics in the classroom. Introducing technology gradually from fifth grade onwards allows students to develop a solid social, emotional, and relational foundation first. This approach can help reduce behaviors like bullying, superficiality, and entitlement.

Inclusivity is another critical aspect that demands attention. The current system often fails to address individual students' diverse learning styles and needs. A more inclusive education system needs to acknowledge and accommodate various learning abilities in ways that benefit children on individual and group levels. Collaboration and consistency must be fostered so every child can thrive according to their skills and the space needed. For some children, this space is sometimes away from the group and sometimes part of the group. Differentiated instructions, personalized learning plans, and increased support for students with diverse needs are essential components of an inclusive educational model. For this model to work, schools need to implement iterative frameworks where learning is tied closely to experimenting, failing is recognized as part of improvement, and the chain of command is replaced with open conversation and speedy implementation. What could this model look like? Restructuring the K-4 curriculum to prioritize building and developing life skills over academic knowledge and eliminating traditional tests and evaluations would establish a solid foundation for inclusivity. This approach would provide children with a different, more inclusive base. Building on this foundation in the classroom would encourage students to pursue goals and outcomes based on their progress, interests, capabilities, and capacity. This approach would naturally foster a willingness to learn and help others learn, making many academic, emotional, social, and behavioral "tools" we currently try to inject into the curriculum unnecessary. Consequently, teachers could transition from authoritarian figures to coaches and collaborators, earning students' respect and connection more efficiently.

The emphasis on standardized testing as a primary measure of success is a significant flaw in the current education system. This approach puts undue pressure on students and educators, promoting a narrow focus on exam preparation at the expense of a broader, more holistic education. A revised system should evaluate students' progress through project-based evaluations, presentations, and practical demonstrations, providing a more comprehensive understanding of their capabilities. I understand that this discussion needs to take place on a larger scale and may require legislative changes, but it should not be overlooked and should be centered around horizontal learning for all. I make it a point of discussion with my daughter before each test she must go through in her classroom that I do not care about the test score, nor should she. What I care about, and so should she, is that she does her best. If her best at that time is less than whatever is considered above average or average, then so be it. I always tell her none of those tests are a measure of how smart she is. There are countless numbers of children, adults even, who are intelligent and resourceful but do not test well. This is why I do not believe in testing but in applying skills, failing, learning, and growing beyond what any test can measure. So, I often remind my daughter that the most important thing is to do her best. To genuinely do her best. Not the best, but her best. I tell her if she follows this, she has already succeeded. That's it. That's all.

Interconnectedness. Academic, social, and emotional learning must be represented better. We need our education system to integrate real-world applications, global perspectives, and interdisciplinary and iterative learning to better prepare our children for the challenges and opportunities they will encounter. The need for this is obvious, yet there is still a disconnect. I believe there is passion and interest among educators in public schools, but the disconnect comes from attempting to run new programs on old systems, and that has a lot to do with mindset. We need to let go of what's not serving our children. I strongly agree it is less effective to knock everything down and start from ground zero than to build on an existing foundation. Why? I also strongly agree that some age-old principles still have relevance and need to be reintroduced in the education system in some shape or form. I'm talking about discipline by a form of discussion and holding space in a way that provides tools for children to learn how to navigate challenges, not discipline by rewarding a specific type of behavior. There are many ways to incorporate this approach. For example, instead of verbally reprimanding a child whose behavior disrupts the classroom or reminding them of a reward they may miss for not behaving correctly, the teacher could pause and briefly inquire about the reason behind the behavior by asking the child to share their thoughts as they relate to the present behavior. The teacher could then involve the class in a supportive brainstorming session with the child, working together to find a helpful solution that restores classroom flow. This process and the outcome of restoring the flow become the reward for the struggling child and the entire class. While this approach takes time, prioritizing life skills in the K-4 curriculum and making academic performance secondary during these years will naturally engage students. It lifts everyone's spirits and helps children develop into kind, strong, decent adults. This approach could be included in a classroom conduct agreement, with teachers and students as the members who adhere to it. The agreement would be developed collaboratively by all classroom members and displayed in a central and easily accessible location in the classroom.

This is just one example. There are many ways to implement this approach. Still, it requires the education system to empower teachers through official training and coaching and to set better parameters for class sizes so teachers can genuinely get to know and work with each child. Another step toward achieving this outcome is to assign a teacher to a group of children (similar to a team) who will provide consistent guidance and coaching from grades K-4. This will change classroom dynamics, strengthen relationships between teachers, students, and parents, and give the children the stability and safety net they need during those years.

I like to observe. What's challenging about observing many times is observing without adding personal thoughts. It isn't easy sometimes, but I consciously avoid mixing my perception with what I observe. I want to give myself enough time to get past an initial internal reaction to the act of observing and allow myself to consider the external for what it is without personally judging. Then, by asking myself questions about what I observed, I can use my thoughts and references to help me arrive at a meaningful conclusion myself without getting too involved in what I'm observing so much so as to become reactive, upset, or somehow directly or indirectly offended. I learned this as an

Agile Coach, which has served me well. A colleague once told me: "Always assume people start with good intentions; things work out much better that way." He was talking about building professional relationships with people. Still, it stayed with me, and I remind myself when I get stuck on a thought, situation, or person. For the past three years, since my daughter started first grade, I've been observing the school environment I send my daughter to and, indirectly, where my nieces and nephews go.

I am consistently noticing this notion that school should be fun for kids to want to go to school. I'm afraid I have to disagree with this. Partially. I'm not convinced that everything needs to be fun to be relevant, that good behavior needs to be rewarded with material prizes, and that the entire academic curriculum is based around each holiday. These are all things that emphasize and encourage children to chase after something, to constantly compete for something, to value instant gratification, comfort, special recognition, etc. These are all things we say should be secondary and shouldn't matter.

On the one hand, children are taught good values through some social and emotional learning programs, but on the other hand, they are practicing something different in the classroom. This is not intentional; it's just not well thought out. A former teacher and a good friend expressed her frustration with our current education system and school practices when she said: "There should be no special recognition for acting as a decent human being." There's no tiptoeing around this issue; it needs to be brought directly to the forefront of the discussion – let's address the elephant in the room. The current state of the PTO concept in schools has resulted in too many cooks in the kitchen. What was meant to enhance the educational experience for children has turned into a party-planning advocacy, bringing the superficial aspects of some holidays into the classroom.

Many productivity books emphasize the importance of associating specific places in your home with specific activities to help your brain build and maintain habits and differentiate between contexts. For example, if I want to relax and unwind with a book, I should find a spot in my home that doesn't remind me of work. Conversely, if I need to be alert and get work done, I should look for an area that puts my brain in work mode. The same principle applies to children in the classroom. The classroom should be a place for learning, not for holding parties. Non-educational matters, parties, and events should be reserved for after school hours at a designated location that is not the classroom. This aspect of the PTO concept needs to be re-evaluated. It has taken a turn for the worse, and at this point, it needs to be mended.

It's hard for a child to learn to consistently behave well if we tie good behavior with a consumption reward. We are conditioning children to behave long enough to get something out of behaving well when, in fact, the behavior itself should be the reward. In essence, we need to help children understand and practice that the good feeling you get from behaving well is the reward. And then elaborate that you get that feeling by helping a classmate, paying attention in class, respecting your elders, and so on. Otherwise, how are children going to grow up and have an appreciation for helping others without being rewarded—without asking, "What's in it for me?" Encouraging children to find intrinsic satisfaction in completing tasks rather than solely focusing on external rewards is fundamental to fostering a growth mindset and long-term motivation. I know many classrooms have toy baskets, and if a child reaches a certain number of points for good behavior, they get to take something from the basket.

Yes, it sounds like fun. But this is short-lived. This encourages the thinking that good behavior should be a temporary act of performance until you get what you want. What happens when there is nothing in it for you? As parents and educators, we must dig deeper before we instill these short-lived practices in the classroom and our homes. We need to do this together by connecting parents and teachers on a child-by-child basis so each child goes through the education years in a team, not alone—a team whose members are the child, the parent, the teacher(s), and the child's classmates.

Shifting perspective in this way contributes to the development of resilience, creativity, and a genuine love for learning. No external reward will ever provide a long-term, meaningful outcome the way teamwork can. And I can't think of a better way to teach children how to be team players but to practice that in the classroom and in real life. The solution is not to implement yet another social-emotional module in classrooms. Instead, we must intentionally shift our focus and practice present-moment mindfulness with our children at home and school. As parents and educators, we must first remind ourselves, and then guide our children, that just because something is momentarily fun doesn't mean it has lasting value. Our goal should be to help children learn and understand how to value things healthily. We live in a culture that prioritizes and promotes short-lived fun and instant gratification; technology only exacerbates this issue. We need to stop! So, what does a solution look like? The first step is to set aside our own "what's in it for me" mindset and come together as parents and educators for a meaningful discussion. The PTO should focus on this activity instead of planning classroom parties.

When children learn to appreciate the journey of tackling a task, they are more likely to engage in activities with enthusiasm and curiosity. A reward-centered approach feels like and encourages a transactional mindset where the primary motivation becomes the desire for external recognition rather than an inherent joy in the process. We need to employ strategies where the value and enjoyment of doing the task are emphasized and valued. So, in the context of academic activities, why not emphasize the inherent satisfaction of problem-solving, the joy of discovery, and the sense of accomplishment that comes from mastering a new skill? By connecting the task to personal growth and learning, children will start associating positive emotions with the process instead of the reward. For example, emphasizing the pleasure of practicing a musical instrument, the camaraderie in team sports, or the satisfaction of creating art encourages children to see these activities as fulfilling on their own. The idea is to create an environment that celebrates effort and resilience. Reinforce the idea that the journey is just as important as the destination. Acknowledging the hard work, perseverance, and creative thinking involved in completing the task develops a sense of pride beyond any external reward. This approach guides children's understanding that challenges are opportunities for growth rather than obstacles in obtaining a reward.

To be able to engage children in meaningful practices at school, I believe we need to emphasize the role of educators in reshaping the education landscape. Professional development opportunities, ongoing training, and teacher support are crucial in ensuring they can effectively implement innovative teaching methods. Also, empowering educators, especially women, as leaders in developing and continuously improving new pedagogical approaches and technologies is essential for achieving accurate, meaningful, scalable, and sustainable education reform. Because that's what we need, an education reform. The type of reform that doesn't just slap an abbreviation to a program but works the program inside and out and adjusts what needs to be adjusted iteratively based on feedback from those who are the closest to the students and without the need for long-drawn approvals dependent on unnecessary chain-of-command structures. This type of education reform is driven by personal and professional capability and continuous and cross-functional collaboration between educators, parents, and children. This type of education reform supports progress, improvement, and collective decision-making. Finally, this type of education reform is on purpose; it excludes all kinds of "hamster wheel" approaches, including competing for the sake of collecting points toward a promotion and rewarding superficial confidence.

The global nature of information and communication requires a renewed emphasis on cultural awareness and global citizenship. Schools must be able to equip our children with the knowledge and skills to engage with diverse perspectives, fostering empathy and developing their own opinions in their own age-appropriate time. Schools must be freed from engaging children in the latest pop-culture happenings and imposing political and controversial agendas onto our children throughout the curriculum. For example, instead of keeping the Santa Lie thriving, children can develop some crucial life skills by learning about the origin of the story of Santa and other similar or different stories across other cultures and then have discussions and projects based on that instead of making their Santa wish list be the project. My child has never owned or walked around with a list of things she wants others to buy her. Not Christmas, not birthday, not anything.

When asked what she wants for these occasions, my daughter answers, "If you want to get something for me, whatever you get will be fine." That's it. You can talk with her and discover what she likes, what she's into, and why. That conversation, that time you spent with her, that attention you gave her, is the present. Why? Because you just learned something about my child. You just connected with her in a meaningful way. Whatever object you give her will be greatly appreciated but short-lived. The object will be put away in a matter of minutes. But she will remember the connection you had with her. This is not the case only with my child. This is the case with any child.

Children are excited about presents because we teach them to be. Seeing the smiles and excitement when they open presents is exciting and fulfilling. But that's because we condition them to do that from day one. If we teach them to get that same smile and excitement from connecting to another human being meaningfully, guess what? They'll deliver on it! Giving and receiving presents is nice. However, they must hold more than a date and a checklist to be genuinely appreciated beyond the expected formal expression of appreciation we deem polite when receiving them. On the other hand, kind, positive connections are forever.

I taught my child to say, "Whatever you get will be fine with me." She had no issues saying that until she started first grade. That's where she learned about Christmas wish lists and birthday wish lists. At first, I would get internally frustrated every time I picked her up from school, and she would share yet another concept that went against our family values. I would practice my "assume everyone starts with good intention" and tell myself there must be a reason why they teach kids at school these things, so I stayed on the down-low during her first year in school. Maybe it's an adjustment for the kids as they try to make sense of this new environment at school. I thought the second year, they'd ease up on these silly activities. Oh my gosh, was I wrong? It got worse! In the third year, I decided to get more involved. I hope to initiate and continue to have meaningful conversations on this topic.

There are a few things I want to mention that deserve some thought and discussion when it comes to making informed, positive changes in the educational landscape. I recognize that educators working directly with students are doing their best with the tools they are given. That is just the thing. Educators (i.e., teachers) need to be given better tools and empowered to be actively involved in designing those tools as they are closest to children. Those with extensive experience know what works and what doesn't. They need to be freed from the constraints they seem to currently be under to perform in a specific way against measures that are difficult to keep up with and sometimes do not make sense. Teachers need to connect with students meaningfully, not through checkboxes and reports. This ties back to the curriculum. Curriculum guidelines are necessary but must also be consistent across schools and school districts. Curriculum guidelines shouldn't be based on various modules that fit individual schools' annual funding perimeters. Education and business need to be separated. Schools should not be paying for curriculum modules. They should be involved in creating and implementing them.

Additionally, education should be kept out of politics. Education policies should not change or be affected by who's in Office. Although this discussion goes beyond the scope of this book, it is a crucial conversation that needs to be had.

Over the past two decades, the education landscape has undergone significant transformations, shaped by technological advancements, shifts in pedagogical approaches, and evolving societal expectations. As a result, a lot of new opportunities have become available. However, the role of the internet, although particularly transformative in how children can access information, has also become a container for all sources of information—credible information and misinformation. Internet usage in schools has created one improvement and, at the same time, opened other challenges. I question the guidelines we use in schools to sort through and identify information versus misinformation or the guidelines used to ensure only age-appropriate content is available to children during school hours. What some parents consider age-appropriate, others may not, and vice versa. So, how do we ensure there is balance? These discussions must occur between parents and educators and between parents and other parents. For example, I was in a situation where I had to initiate a conversation with one of my child's teachers to remove some content a child in the classroom was allowed to watch to reward good behavior. My concern was that the content chosen by one student was played for the entire class, and the content was not what I would allow my eight-year-old to watch at home. But, because no other parent complained, nothing was done until I initiated a conversation. I was mind-boggled by the fact that this is our reality. The school didn't have specific guidelines in place to prevent content that is not age-appropriate from being shown as part of the norm in the classroom. This is just one example.

In a conversation with a parent of a kindergartener in another school district, I learned about two similar incidents where inappropriate content was played in the classroom. A parent had to complain to the teacher to remove it. Incidents like these demonstrate the need for more agile practices in education, including iterative learning processes, accountability-based involvement, and improvements based on constructive failures. This includes more parent-student-teacher involvement. Although progress has been made towards more student-centered and interactive learning approaches in the classroom, I still believe there needs to be more personalized communication between parents and educators. On the other side, I think that there is a greater emphasis on collaborative learning, project-based activities, and discussions that engage students to be active participants in the learning process, and that is encouraging because that's what contributes to nurturing critical thinking, creativity, and problem-solving skills essential for success in a rapidly changing world. At the same time, we need to see more rapid improvements in how these concepts are applied in the educational landscape across school districts. As previously mentioned, there shouldn't be such significant gaps between how different school districts operate. This is so mind-boggling to me, and it just does not make sense that school districts within the same state operate under different umbrellas, and they seem to be almost competing against each other by being ranked.

It's encouraging that assessment methods, in most instances, are no longer limited to traditional tests and exams. Instead, there is an effort to recognize the need for a more comprehensive evaluation that includes various assessment tools. However, project-based assessments, portfolios, presentations, and even gamified assessments, although increasing, I still don't believe provide a sufficient level of holistic understanding of children's abilities and potential. On the flip side, diverse learning styles and recognition of individual differences have become more pronounced. Two decades ago, there was a tendency to adopt a one-size-fits-all approach to education, with limited accommodations for varying learning needs. Today, there is a greater awareness of the importance of differentiated student instruction. Educators strive to tailor their teaching methods to accommodate different learning styles and provide additional support for students with diverse needs, fostering a more inclusive and equitable educational environment. However, schools must be mindful of how these methods are implemented, how they affect all the students in the classroom, and the effect on the student(s) whose attributes may not be represented among their classmates. These students may feel included, but it may add stress to their ability to function off a baseline that is not aligned with the rest of their classmates. The rest of the classmates may find their classroom environment an unstable place to be and develop a level of stress that can affect academic performance and social and emotional struggles that spill over into their daily lives outside the classroom.

I strongly advocate for lifelong learning because it is a valuable growth mindset for our children. This concept goes beyond traditional education, encompassing a broader scope of knowledge that continues throughout life. Adopting this educational strategy properly can transform how we leverage modern technological advancements in schools. This transformation is crucial for equipping our children to navigate the fast-evolving job markets they will face as adults. These changes challenge current approaches to education and call for the need to pause and question the value of our children's current social and academic growth beyond what's on the surface. These changes call for digging deep and reshaping the current education landscape. These are changes that call for ripping the band-aid. On the surface, progress is made by trying to keep up with current technology, and that's great. But what's the value in that for children? Because it can't just be going along with technology. We are all experiencing and will continue to experience the adverse effects of the way we use technology. In the context of the educational topography, are we implementing technology to say we are in check with it, or are we implementing technology in a targeted manner to solve a problem? There are many times when I question what problem we are solving by introducing some of these aspects of technology in the classroom when our children don't know how to write cursive (not type, write). My daughter's first and second-grade homework did not include handwriting exercises. Still, children were given Chromebooks to learn through on-screen exercises mimicking video games because that is supposed to make learning fun. I work in information technology, and I still find this off-putting. Technology needs to serve us, but I continuously observe that we serve technology.

We are constantly implementing and updating new technologies and changing how we operate to align with new tools. Tools are great if they serve a purpose other than novelty. The prevalence of screens and digital devices has raised questions about the impact on students' attention spans, mental health, and social interactions. How not surprising, yet how undermined! Striking a balance between leveraging technology for educational benefits and mitigating its potential drawbacks is a crucial challenge for educators, parents, and children. This needs to be addressed much faster and bolder than it currently is. Let's have that conversation. Now. Because it's already becoming too late. We are in treating mode when we should be preventing all this.

Alongside implementing and continuously updating technology in the classroom and at home, we need to develop techniques and practices that build a sense of autonomy and ownership in how our children operate as individuals and as part of a group. When children have a say in their tasks and can approach them in ways that align with their interests and strengths, they are more likely to find intrinsic motivation. However, for this to work, children need structure at home, structure at school, and a lot less information overload. We must provide the environment for them to discover instead of opening the door to everything out there all at once. To provide this environment and give our children a standing chance at autonomy that helps them see the value in the process (not the reward in the form of a physical object), we must pose the why question every step of the way for every technological implementation. Then, we need to teach our children to question technological implementation every step of the way! Building new technology is fun and can exist for the sole purpose of existing, but implementing built technologies and using these new technologies with children needs to include a significant level of supervision and guidance.

Something I do with my child now is have continuous and consistent discussions before any technological exposure. Now that she is nine, she can use a tablet for a limited time and particular purposes. For example, she enjoys drawing, so she can use an app that helps her practice that skill. Anything entertainment-related must go through a different process. That process goes like this: first, she tells me what it is – a movie, a song, a game, etc., and then, I ask her what she knows about it. Then, I check it out to determine if it's appropriate for her. Once I do that, I share my findings with her and explain why I think it's okay or not for her to consume. At this point, she has a few options: she can ask more questions, share her opinion if she disagrees with my decision, or, if my answer is still no, we discuss the appropriate age to consume the movie, show, etc.

I used this approach extensively with movies and TV shows before other electronic devices came into the picture, and it has worked well. It has helped her reason, learn patience, and stay persistent about what she wants. When she started first grade, she asked if she could watch two TV shows that I did not consider age-appropriate for her then. The answer for both shows was a hard no; I told her we could reconsider when she was at least ten years old. Instead of getting upset and whining about it, she initiated our discussion process. Through discussions and debates, she eventually decided she didn't even want to watch one of the shows but was still very interested in watching the other one. This kind of attitude and ability to carry a discussion earned her enough maturity points for me to allow her to watch the one she was still interested in a year earlier than initially stated, with the condition that we watch it together. She agreed. The excitement and happiness she expressed is something I will never forget and something she would not have experienced, and I would not have witnessed it if I had just given in and said, "Well, if everyone at school watched it, then we should too." The small things we fail to practice always make the most significant difference.

I often wonder why parents and children are not included in the development of school curriculums. Voting by committee does not fit every time, but involvement in the process and consideration of ideas from the people these programs are supposed to serve is common sense. For example, why aren't we implementing programs in early grades that strengthen the parent-child-teacher relationship? Why don't we standardize programs that call for capability-based mastermind groups where, throughout the school year, the teacher holds regular 15-minute calls with each child and at least one of the parents? During these calls, the child, with the help of the parent(s), can set personal goals and preferences for the year and watch their progress throughout these personal child accountability calls. Of course, these sessions will be age-appropriate. I can almost guarantee positive outcomes as each child practices how to question what's in front of them and make decisions based on how a decision aligns with their personal goals and preferences. Now, that life skill will set a child up for success!

Something I am very aware of in any situation is the fact that children often mirror the attitudes and behaviors of the adults in their lives. This can be pretty intimidating and, at times, hard to accept, but as truth has it, it simply is. Whether you find it offensive or see it as an opportunity to grow, it remains the truth. I have felt this truth slap in my face a couple of times as a parent, and I am most honestly grateful for it because it has humbled me and helped me grow in my role. I'm still learning, and I will continue to learn. This truth can be harsh when a child demonstrates lousy behavior, especially the type of bad behavior their parent(s) have addressed theoretically but not followed through practically. It hurts. It can be unpleasant. It can be downright angering. But it will remain the truth until I decide to adjust, and the truth reflects my adjustments.

As a parent, I must model a healthy relationship for my child. Not a superficially healthy relationship. A healthy relationship with all the challenges and setbacks that come along with it. My husband and I make significant efforts to model for our daughter a mindset that values the process, embraces mistakes as learning opportunities, and persists through difficulties so she can adopt a similar attitude. I said significant efforts because sometimes, for some topics, this comes naturally, while other times, it takes a considerable amount of effort. And make no mistake, we have failed and continue to fail; that's just the thing: failing means we are actively working on things. Failing means spending time together as we determine our next step, action, and approach. This builds an unbreakable bond among us and helps our daughter learn essential life skills by experiencing, experimenting, failing, getting up, learning, failing again, and improving, never perfecting but constantly improving because improvement is just so much better than perfection (whatever that turns out to be)! I highly doubt any technological approach in any shape or form (including artificial intelligence) will be able to work with a child in this way. To this extent, below, I share my AgileParenting™ strategies and tools as I use them with my child. Take what resonates; leave what doesn't.

I encourage curiosity and exploration. I use open-ended questions to help my daughter practice critical thinking. Early on, I implemented a *let's do a project* time with my daughter, where we both worked on the same thing or created our version of whatever we would be drawing, building, or sculpting. During these project sessions, I've heard some of my daughter's most incredible wisdom.

I promote autonomy and decision-making. My daughter is included in the decision-making in our household. She understands her input is always considered and, when appropriate, included in our decision-making. She also understands her feelings, and her suggestions are valid and valued even when we must decide the opposite of what she has proposed. We ensure our daughter understands that being genuine, honest, and transparent among the three of us is more important than being right and getting things your way. I have been discussing the topic of age-appropriate content with my daughter very early on, including why she must stay within the content boundaries we set for her. I discovered early on that my child can be pretty reasonable if I explain why I'm asking something of her or not allowing her something. She got it if I allowed her to process my explanation herself, even as a toddler. This was a great discovery for me as a parent and has been a blessing! Sometimes, I don't feel like explaining: I feel more like, "Do as I say because I said it." During those times, I'm very transparent with her, and I say that I feel irritated and that it has nothing to do with her but that I need a minute to reset. She usually says: "Aha, got it." Then I take that minute. As soon as I'm back and all collected, I dive into the why of whatever we're trying to figure out. By doing this, I am giving her tools to cope in situations when she doesn't feel one hundred percent. I am modeling that it's okay not always to be calm, collected, and ready, but it's not OK to dump my attitude onto someone else just because I'm not in a good mood. I am giving her the tools to recognize situations, differentiate attitudes, and make decisions independently when my husband and I are not close by to explain. The best way for any child to get that is through parent modeling. At this age, it involves deciding what to do if another kid displays verbal or physical behavior that she knows is not considered age-appropriate in our household. Or to recognize a friend's mean attitude as something the friend is having a hard time with and not take it personally. Or even yet to identify times when it is personal and that friend may not be a friend after all. When a situation like this presents itself, we have extensive discussions afterward as she usually has a million and one questions. Still, at the moment, she is equipped to make her own decisions. This is a continuous practice, and it's not perfect, but it is good enough to set a foundation. I can't protect her from everything in the external world, but I can keep the communication open so she can be equipped enough to navigate through all the noise.

I emphasize learning in the learning process. I always highlight the importance of the journey and the existing and learned skills because of the journey. My daughter understands that results are good, but the process matters more. Many times, we don't even spend much time on the result. For example, I refrain from asking how she did on a test and instead, I ask how she felt during the test and what she found interesting, challenging, easy, etc. I never ask about the grades or points they use in schools these days to measure the level of smartness in my daughter until she brings it up or gives me the paper from her teacher. She must take these MAP tests a few times throughout the year. She brought this last one home on a Friday and didn't show me until Monday after school. I don't care for any of those numbers and percentages they try to attach to my child's development. I keep telling my daughter to focus on doing her best, learn from her failures, and keep improving at her own pace. That's the only measure of anything in her development. As I tell her, everything else is just noise and potential distraction, including grades. Because I know if she does her best and embraces lifelong learning as a mindset, she'll get through school and be more than okay—she'll be her best!

I provide constructive feedback. Not everything my child does or makes will be tremendous and deemed exceptional. However, I have always given her positive feedback, focusing on her efforts and improvement since the last time. But before giving her feedback, I always ask for her evaluation. It's incredible how honest kids can be with themselves if we let them lead the conversation instead of influencing their reaction by instantly reacting ourselves. They even develop their solutions if we listen and minimally guide the discussion. As a parent, watching it unfold before my eyes is amazingly refreshing. All we must do is listen. Hmm… Who knew, right?

I set realistic expectations. Through discussions timed appropriately, I help my daughter understand that to me, as her mother, everything she presents will be tremendous and memorable but that the external world may not always agree with me. And that's ok. I tell her her goal is never to please. Her goal is to grow, create, and be who she is, with the understanding that the external world will not always agree. Still, if she understands right from wrong, is honest about what's real and imagined, and puts her best out there, the world will either shrink in irrelevance or expand in support.

I eliminate external rewards. I encourage my child to reflect on her accomplishments, not just her shortcomings. I do not attach external rewards to accomplishments. Instead, I ask her to talk about what is happening or what happened internally before, during, and after an accomplishment or a shortcoming, and through discussion, she arrives at the joy she feels from experiencing the process that led to her accomplishment or the lesson she can take with her from a shortcoming. My husband and I sometimes use an external reward; it's never attached to the behavior directly, and it's not an actual physical object like a toy. It's a general celebration of something and more of an experience rather than just a transactional act. For example, we could say, "It's a nice day, and we haven't had ice cream in a while. Let's get some ice cream." I don't ask her to do something so she can have ice cream as a reward. In another instance, we may say, "You know, you've been working hard on that song for the past week. Let's take a break and celebrate how far you've come by doing something you'd like. What would you like to do?" Usually, it's going to her favorite restaurant (we don't eat out much) or going to an art place called "Color-Me-Mine" or ordering pizza and having a movie night—although we have movie nights every Friday—I guess they don't get old. She very rarely associates such celebrations with toys. It's usually the experience she goes for.

9

Parenting in the Age of Information Overload

From Online Influence to Informed Choices: We Must Shift Now!

In the internet and social media age, teaching my child the concepts of right versus wrong has become increasingly complex and challenging. It has also become that much more crucial. The vast, openly available information online is diverse and highly influenced by social media. Therefore, the erosion of traditional moral authorities spreads at lightning speed. This informs me that my priority is helping my child develop critical thinking skills. More and more, concepts such as freedom of speech, freedom of expression, open mindset, and acceptance are dangerously close to replacing basic moral principles, attitudes, and individual and societal responsibility. Instead of being used as values to complement, enhance, and make for a strong society, such concepts are marketed and promoted with an underlying agenda of anything and everything goes. The more out of the ordinary, the better.

As an Agile Coach, I discuss the importance of change and responding to change. I am very much pro-change and -improvement. I believe it's essential to make progress on an individual and societal level by re-evaluating our values and principles so we can evolve as individuals and as a people. I also believe change for the sake of change is a recipe for disaster. Understanding the change's purpose is crucial to any implementation process. To understand,

and I mean truly understand, the why behind any undertaking, we need to dig deep and expand our vision beyond the immediate outcomes. There is a phrase we use in my line of work that says the presenting problem is never the actual problem. So, standing on the sidelines observing the changes we are after as a society and the way we go about these changes, I can't help but ask, what's the purpose? Because it all feels forced, superficial, and borderline morally questionable.

For better or worse (and it seems it's headed for worse), social media has way too much influence on the lives of young individuals, and as time goes by, it continues to claim younger and younger victims. At times, this constant baggage from social media feels like carefully crafted organized chaos in the making. This is another reason, and arguably a top priority reason, why the role of the mother as the central adult figure in a child's life is so much needed today. Today, more than ever, mothers need to stay home because they need to fight against the overwhelming external world that's after our children! The first two years of a child's development and the continuous close guidance beyond those years can make or break that child's ability to progress. Exposure to non-age-appropriate concepts can initially seem harmless and funny but is later pinpointed as the starting point for more significant life problems. The problem is that what's considered age-appropriate these days is shifting, again in the name of free speech, free expression, and freedom to do whatever because everything must be accepted and encouraged. There are fewer and fewer consequences to our actions because almost everything can be justified under the umbrella of being free to act/do/be as I choose. I love progress; I'm sad about how we go about it. So, how do I approach the concept of right versus wrong with my child? Every year, it seems to get more challenging because more and more is being thrown in our faces. So once again, I rely on my AgileParenting™ framework and remind myself of my parenting why. Reminding myself why I choose every day to be the kind of parent I am helps me stay focused on what I committed to before I even became a mother and the promise I made to myself of how I will show up for my child. It's not easy. But it's the right thing to do. I approach my parenting from four focus areas, as laid out below.

Overwhelming Access to Information. The internet is a double-edged sword when educating my child about moral and ethical issues. On one hand, it provides access to a wealth of information and diverse viewpoints that can enrich my child's understanding of the world. On the other hand, the sheer volume of information, not all of which is age-appropriate or factually accurate, can overwhelm her mind as a child. Conflicting messages about what is considered right or wrong, more often than we like to admit, lead to confusion and difficulty in discerning reliable from unreliable sources, therefore blurring the line between what's real and what's not, what's true and what's not. My approach? I eliminated electronic device usage and knowledge of the content any of these devices held for the first five years of my daughter's life. My child didn't know a phone could be anything but an object to call people on and take pictures.

When my daughter started kindergarten, due to the pandemic, she had to use a laptop or an iPad to attend class virtually. Beyond the required Zoom time, she had no access to any other apps on my iPad, and once the class was done, so was her exposure to the screen. When the class ended, the iPad was put away. I didn't even care to sift through content and figure out what was age-appropriate for my child. At that age, everything regarding the online world was off-limits. She learned what she needed to learn from me from physical books, board games, and highly filtered content on TV that we watched together. Yes, I sat and watched Mickey Mouse Clubhouse with my daughter and had discussions with her on questions she had, laughed with her on parts she found funny (and sometimes I didn't find that funny), and answered her questions. It was during this activity that I learned how curious my child is. I would not have known or learned this if not for the time I spent with her. Learning this early on helped me better understand her personality and guide and encourage her development accordingly. It made for strengthening our bond.

Social Media Influence. Social media platforms have transformed the landscape of interpersonal communication and community engagement. Unfortunately for children—and adolescents—these platforms are not just sources of information; they are significant tools for socialization and influence. This influence has very quickly turned negative in the form of cyberbullying, misinformation, and the display of unrealistic lifestyles and values. The prevalence of these negative factors poses challenges in teaching right versus wrong, skewing a child's perception of normalcy, morality, and ethics. Choosing to stay awake and not take part while watching these pathways being planted by social media is extremely difficult, sad, and quite discouraging. In my opinion, the lack of regulations or even basic guidelines on what is morally and ethically acceptable to share with the world represents a misuse of our freedom and a clear example of irresponsibility on a widespread scale.

Just because "anything" is possible doesn't mean anything should be accepted and displayed. My approach? I have a brain reset session with my child every day after school. I hold space for her to tell me everything about the happenings at school during the day, the things she learned, the things she found odd, the things she didn't quite 'get,' and anything else she would like to share with me. Then I start point by point, to break down and dissect each concept, topic, idea, event, and perception, and reset her mind back to her center. I do this so she can start from her center the next day, not where the external world left her off. Sometimes, she will not tell me something until a day or two later. That's because sometimes she needs time to process things independently and then come to me. That is perfectly fine because she and I have already established trust that she comes to me first, whatever the matter is. So, I trust she will come to me first when ready to articulate whatever she is going through. She knows this because it is reiterated in our household that whatever it is, good, bad, and anything in between, she comes to me and my husband first. If she seeks answers, she comes to us first. Not her best friend, not her other friends, not her teacher, not anyone but us first. She can get perspective from the external world and form her own opinion, but she comes to us first. This is not practiced with children nearly as much as it should be. Helping my child understand this, not just by memorizing it but also by understanding why it's important that she comes to us first, is the 101 of all 101s regarding her defense against social media.

The intention is to help her understand that her source is never the external world. Instead, it is her inner circle, her parents, and her family. For better or worse, I have promised myself that I will do my absolute best to ensure I will not serve my child to the system—especially not the broken system we live in today! What does that mean? This means that our child-raising system today is shaky at best. I fought for this child of mine for an entire decade. I will not raise her by chance. I will give her my best because that's what she deserves. That's what every child deserves.

Now, I am very aware that every day, she is becoming a person with her own opinions and beliefs and that she will make her own decisions that, many times, I will have to disagree with. I already practice decision-making with her, and she has made a few decisions that I almost crushed (pun intended), but I didn't. Instead, I observed. There have been times when a decision she's made would work out great, even better than what I had in mind. I acknowledge that with her through a discussion, and I hold space for her to express how she feels about her accomplishment—no reward is provided other than accepting the good feeling that comes with that accomplishment—that's her reward. There have been times when her decision would not yield the best outcome. I also acknowledge that with her through a discussion, and I hold space for her to express how she feels and what she intends to do next. One thing she and I like to do after an accomplishment is to express and celebrate our feelings by doing a happy dance. Even after a failure, we do a happy dance as soon as we've expressed how we feel and figured out the lesson from the failure, no matter how big or small that lesson is.

Traditional Moral Authorities. Traditionally, institutions such as families, schools, and religious organizations played central roles in imparting moral values to children. However, the authority of these institutions has been increasingly questioned or undermined in the digital era. The internet provides alternative narratives and communities that may conflict with the moral teachings from these traditional sources. As a result, children may experience confusion or adopt values that diverge from those of their families or communities. My approach? I combine elements of traditional and modern parenting. I ensure some old values are not lost while more modern views are considered and implemented accordingly. I guide my child to respect everyone, especially older people. We talk about respect a lot. We talk about the difference between how she can speak with friends and how she can speak with adults and why it matters to be respectful in that way. For example, I've heard some adults emphasize how a child addresses them (by their first name vs. their last name). I don't care if my child addresses an adult by their first name or designated title in society if she understands and knows how to be respectful. It doesn't matter if a child addresses me as Mrs. Dimovski if, beyond that address, that same child is disrespectful to me and uses inappropriate language with me. I'd much rather have a child call me Bia but respect me enough not to talk back to me or use inappropriate language. On the flip side of respect, I guide my child to always stand up for herself and speak up no matter who's in front of her. The only rule is she must do so in a respectful way.

Critical Thinking Skills. One of the key challenges in guiding my child through what's right versus wrong in the digital age is developing essential skills of thinking or what I like to call common sense. Yes, common sense is something you can be born with, but you can also learn if you choose to. With the abundance of information and perspectives available online, I find it crucial for my child to learn early how to evaluate sources' credibility, understand different viewpoints, and make informed judgments. Of course, this is not a one, two, three method; it takes time, and it must be set at a different pace based on each child's needs and personality, which is another reason why I chose to stay home with my child during the most crucial years in her development and remain closely involved in her life during her school years thus far. Working with children to develop common sense requires a proactive approach, both formally in a classroom setting and informally in a home setting. However, it must start at home. The classroom is not the source of a child's development; the classroom is just one pillar. This is why it is so vital that we actively work together to change the educational landscape and protect our children from what's not serving them. Social media and pop culture are not serving them! Yet many schools keep trying to modernize teaching styles by introducing pop culture, social media references, and even content in the classroom. They encourage free expression to the point of kids showing up to school dressed completely inappropriately and even carrying a sense of pride that they are bold enough to do that because "who cares what others think? This is me, and this is how I like to express myself." There is little consideration for time and place. This mindset and attitude leaves little room for respect for others, concern for common sense, and consideration for appropriateness. Everything seems to be appropriate. This notion suggests that if you're not on the 'anything goes' social wagon, you're close-minded, old-school, and narrow in your views.

My approach is zero social media exposure at home. She's brought anything she knows about social media and all the apps, like TikTok and Messenger, Instagram and Facebook, and whatever else is and will pop up overnight, from her classmates at school. Yes, from school. From kids and teachers at school. It was challenging for me as a parent before, but it's been triple challenging after she started school to protect my child against the external world, specifically social media. I considered homeschooling her for a while, but my husband and I eventually decided to opt out of homeschooling as we were concerned about the socializing factor because although I work from home, both of us work full-time, so there would not be sufficient time for scheduling homeschooling and social activities. Instead, I have long and deep conversations with her about every little new piece of information she brings home that she hears from a friend at school. We discuss the pros and cons of the content and the context until she has a solid understanding of whatever information was prematurely thrown at her because "what's the harm? They'll learn anyway." Sure, but how a seven-year-old child processes data meant for a sixteen-year-old will have different implications and outcomes on that child's life as an individual. I put a lot of effort into helping my daughter understand why it's not okay for her to follow/copy specific trends and friends. Sure, she'll eventually decide for herself. Still, until she reaches that level of maturity, I am put here to be the adult in her life who will guide her because there is a difference between learning about something at age seven and learning the same thing at age 17. That's why the concept of age-appropriate keeps shifting by the minute toward a mindset that everything is out in the open and readily available, so everything must be equally appropriate for all ages.

Addressing these challenges requires consistent effort from parents, educators, and policymakers. Parents can engage in open and honest discussions with their children about the content they encounter online; they can set boundaries for internet use and model ethical behavior. But what if parents need education and help in how to parent? Educators can incorporate media literacy into the curriculum, teach students how to critically assess the information they encounter, and understand the impact of social media on society and individual perceptions of right and wrong. But what if educators need to be educated on how to do all that? Policymakers can contribute by supporting initiatives that promote digital literacy and ensure safer online environments for children. But what if policymakers need to be educated on meaningful and purposeful decision-making? We need to start asking more profound questions. Questions that go beyond what's on the surface. And we need to start developing solutions that serve something more than fun and last longer than the present moment. A while ago, I read in a book that the Native Americans had a philosophy that they lived by, which dictated that every decision they made today not only needed to consider how beneficial it is for the current generation but also how it will affect people seven generations out. Can we even fathom that? We can barely consider the next generation as we are all wrapped up in a "look at me, it's all about me" digital era mindset.

I stand by what I say when I say modeling open communication and trust with children is a foundational aspect of building strong, healthy relationships. This sounds good, and on the surface, we all agree with it. But how are we implementing it? What is our support system in implementing it? I am implementing as much as possible with my child, but I shouldn't feel like I'm going against the grain. And I am going against the grain. I have been told many times. On one hand, I have been told I'm too involved with my child.

On the other hand, I have been complimented for my child's behavior and outlook on life. It's hard. But I'm going to keep my hard. My hard involves demonstrating behaviors that encourage my child to express her thoughts, feelings, and experiences openly and without fear of judgment or repercussion, but also appropriately and with a purpose, never just for the sake of expressing, never for the sake of getting attention; and never at the cost of someone else or due to someone else's demand. Below, I share key strategies and principles from the AgileParenting™ framework I use to model open communication and trust with my child.

Lead by Example. I value my child's words by giving her undivided attention, making eye contact, nodding, and responding honestly without overly praising or not giving enough praise. I actively listen to her first, and then I openly express my own emotions and thoughts in an age-appropriate manner. If I feel frustrated or irritated, I tell her at the beginning of the conversation so we decide to continue or to pin the conversation for a later time. Then, I will make sure to follow up at a later time. It works great!

Create a Safe Environment. I establish trust with my child by never promising anything. I always say maybe or let me think about it. If I do make a promise, it is about something I know I can deliver on. I never promise something for the sake of the moment or situation in exchange for good behavior. That way, she knows she can't return to me later with "you promised." She tried that once. As she said, "You promised," I looked her straight in the eyes; she paused, looked at me for a second, and started cracking up because she knew her response was simply invalid (Mommy doesn't promise anything). Part of creating this safe environment for my child is every time she starts a sentence with "I want to tell you something but…" I ensure I reiterate that she can tell me anything, and I will never get upset because I heard it from her. I tell her the only time I will get upset is if it has something to do with her, and she's had the opportunity to share with me before I found out from someone else, but she didn't. I also reiterate that any questions I may have will be asked to understand the situation better and not judge her or anyone else.

Facilitate Open Dialogue. I ask open questions. I often ask my daughter to elaborate on her thoughts and feelings by asking questions that cannot be answered with a simple "yes" or "no." Sometimes, my daughter needs some time to process something before she comes to me for answers. I am patient and available. The only rule is that she comes to me as soon as she's ready and does not wait too long. The reason is that the sooner she comes to me with a problem, the sooner I can help her, and she will not have to carry around a burden. Because burdens tend to get progressively heavier the longer we keep them to ourselves. I tell her it's important to share such burdens but not just with anyone—with the right people, and my husband and I will always be the right people for her!

Embrace Emotional Intelligence. I did an exercise with my daughter when she was around three years old. She and I named emotions, and as we gave them names, she did the facial expressions for each emotion. I took pictures of each facial expression she made, and then we both went through the pictures and talked about each expression. She loved it. It was fun to hear her talking about each emotion. She even gave examples for some of them within a three-year-old frame of reference. I intended to guide her to think of emotions as something to be expressed and something that comes and goes. I continue that conversation as prompted to this day, reminding her that it is imperative to feel her emotions fully and equally important not to dwell on them for too long. Experience it fully (right time and place). Take your time to sit in it. Then move on.

Respect Privacy and Boundaries. I work with my daughter on how to set boundaries, recognize and clearly articulate when she feels those boundaries are not respected, and firmly demand respect for her boundaries when needed. Just like her feelings and experiences are valid, so are her boundaries. We often discuss how important it is that her path is hers and doesn't need to look or feel like someone else's path. Sometimes, I don't understand or agree with her perspective, but I acknowledge it and try to learn from her.

Encourage Independence. This is an ongoing practice in our household. Before we decide on something that involves all three of us, each of us makes our point, and then we decide as a group. If my daughter brings up something that concerns her directly, we ask her to choose first, and if she feels she needs our feedback, we provide it. If it stretches toward her safety and well-being, we would clearly state why we're taking over and why this is a mommy/daddy decision, even though it's about her directly. Everything is discussed and explained at length. One such discussion was about a ride she wanted to go on, but we said no. Problem-solving is also part of encouraging my daughter to be independent. I introduced the concept of improvisation to my daughter through play and project building. Improvise was perhaps the third word she learned how to say. We've improvised on projects since she was two years old. It's so much fun, and it enhances her creativity.

Offer Unconditional Support. There is one thing I make sure my child knows: I'm there for her no matter what! I even make sure I check in with her from time to time to reiterate, plus I love hearing her response. During the most recent check-in, she smiled and said, "I know, I know, you are! And I know how much you love me, too!" Then she'll walk a few steps away from me, turn, and say with a smile, "I love you too!"

10
My Agile Parenting Approach

Balancing Intentionality and Flexibility

Agile Parenting™ is a parenting style based on iterative learning for both child and parent. This requires a change in perspective regarding the various parent-child relationship theories we are accustomed to and those we are so keen to throw out of practice, dismissing them as dated. Agile Parenting™ is founded on the importance of parenting according to specific values that never go out of style (or shouldn't) that, if implemented as intended, are universal and a good starting and anchoring approach to parenting. Here's what's interesting about this framework I developed. The framework itself is not a novel idea. It's based on a framework used in software development to form teams and define processes that set the team up for success. For the team to be successful, everyone on the team needs to be successful at different times in different instances. This framework, when appropriately implemented, does not fail to account for the individual and the team. I came across this framework when I returned to work after over three and a half years of staying home with my child. Returning to work meant doing something that offered enough flexibility to still be present with my child during the day and excel professionally. Yes, I put this out, and I started to actively reach out and make connections that eventually led me to the role of an Agile Coach. I am sharing this with you because it was at this time that I discovered the Agile methodology and one of the frameworks within that methodology, the Scrum framework. This is the framework I used as inspiration in developing my parenting framework.

I decided to share this framework publicly because it works when used as intended and because I have been asked about my approach to parenting. Still, I have only been able to provide small glimpses that don't paint the whole picture. So, this is my attempt to offer what I discovered and experienced as a parent in the past eight years of my child's life. Some may see this as a gift from a fellow parent; others may find it insignificant. Either way, you'll get a different perspective or find the confidence you need to know that you are not the only parent out there who thought of parenting the way you do. What I am sharing in the following pages is so simple to comprehend yet can be challenging to implement precisely because of everything else I touched on in this book. Here it goes.

I did not create the Agile Parenting™ framework before becoming a mother. Although I had a lot of time to think about my potential parenting approach, I didn't have this framework ready to go before having my child. It came together over a few years into my parenting experience. I decided very early into my fertility journey that I wanted to be intentional in raising my child. As an analogy, I didn't want to run around like I do in the kitchen when I try to follow a recipe because it never really turns out right (for me). I'm terrible in the kitchen, and I'm not joking; ask around! I felt as much as I was great with kids and as much as I wanted to have them on my own, parenting would be new to me, something I'd never done before. For many parents (me included), parenting can sometimes feel like you are following a recipe for making a birthday cake, but when you open the oven, a whole bunch of little cupcakes comes out instead of a cake. Would I experience parenting the way I experience the kitchen? If baking comes naturally to you, all this sounds ridiculous, but the anxiety is real if you are not a natural at baking or cooking! To me, the role of a parent was always something I wanted and felt genuinely fulfilling. I just hadn't done it before.

I had quite some time to ponder what parenting would look like for me, landing on *intentional,* which perhaps isn't much of a surprise or a novelty coming from me; it simply fits the profile. Following this line of thought, intentional parenting is a mindset I shifted toward, while Agile Parenting™ is a framework I use to fall back on any time I feel lost or overwhelmed in my role as a parent. Yes, that happens from time to time. It doesn't mean I'm failing as a parent. It simply means I need to fall back on the appropriate element of my parenting framework. You may be wondering (or not, but I'll tell you anyway) how I used this framework and why. I mean, what's the connection? Some business approach to software development processes and parenting? It sounds a bit 'stiff' – is that the word?

Having a child has been the most fulfilling experience of my life. Nothing comes close to it, and I doubt anything ever will! Would I have been unfulfilled without this experience in my life? I can't say for sure because I eventually got pregnant and had my sweet, fantastic, amazing daughter. However, I find the timing of the events pretty interesting. Years later, I still can't correctly articulate that to myself… But I can convey the deep gratitude that settled in me when I held my little girl in my arms! That is crystal clear. It's been eight years, and that sense of gratitude has remained as solid as the day my child was born. Since then, I have found proof that gratitude ignites fulfillment every day. And that's pretty awesome! Even though it took me a while to realize this.

Having my child was the most fulfilling experience! Staying home to raise my child was the best decision I have ever made! It wasn't all peaches and cream. It was hard. It was tight, financially and, many times, emotionally. It was chaotic and not at all according to plan! But waking up every day to the first thought, "I'm a mom," was unbelievably amazing! I. Am. A. Mom. I gave birth to the most amazing human being I have ever met and have the privilege to know.

I became immersed in motherhood, raising my child the best possible way I knew how. That was all that mattered. My love for my child. My child in my arms. That was all for me. At the same time, I struggled with what that 'best' really meant. Sometimes, I felt I was doing it all wrong – no 'undo' button was in sight. But staying home with my child and spending time with her all day every day led me to redefine my sense of self as a parent, as an individual, as a wife, and as a professional – every role I felt was fading during my infertility. This brought a full circle of events, resulting in an immense and steady burst of fulfilling energy that continues to evolve. Words cannot express how forever grateful I am for all of it!

If you look up the definition of Agile, you will find it is "…characterized by the division of tasks into short phases of work and frequent reassessment and adaptation of plans." There are different frameworks to use when adopting this methodology, including the Scrum framework. The Scrum framework helps teams structure and manage their work through values, principles, and practices. Why am I telling you all this? Becoming a Scrum Master and coaching teams and individuals through Agile transformations helped me rethink my approach to parenting. See, my vocation path led me to some pretty amazing people who understood my path and encouraged me to continue to grow with them, as part of their company and as an individual. That is rare! Even now, with the collective work-life balance mindset shift, as we have started experimenting with over the last couple of years. Because of this turn of events, I was able to continue to be fully immersed in my role as a mother and fully immersed in my role as a Professional Scrum Master. There were many times I would be working, and my child would be on my lap, next to me at the desk, or right by me on the floor. There were numerous virtual calls she was on as a non-vocal participant. She seemed to have absorbed much of the content during those meetings – more than I thought she would or could! :)

After running this ship for a while, I noticed my child started using some vocabulary I would use with my teams during my calls. What was incredible was that she started using some of the terminology I used during my meetings to describe concepts in her world. She was using that terminology in the correct context. And it hit me! I realized that the methods, techniques, and tools I used while working with teams made perfect sense to my daughter! That's why she could use some pretty big words in the correct context. So, I decided to put this theory to the test! I started using the methods, techniques, and tools from my work environment with my daughter in different situations to explain things about the world around her that were all new and ready to be discovered and interpreted. It worked! The incredible thing about this experience is that my role as a parent and a professional

Scrum Master/Agile Coach have merged most beautifully. Even with all the scientific and technological advances in our world that push us to believe we hold the ultimate power, every day, I find proof that we are not at all that powerful and that God works in mysterious ways. Everyone's path is different. Would I be saying the same thing I said had I had a different infertility ending? It would be pretty arrogant of me to say yes or no with certainty because I can only speak to the experience I went through. I don't know what my life would have looked like had I experienced a different ending to my infertility story or if I would at all be sharing any of it with you. That would be like reading a book and then asking the author to rewrite the book with a different ending. They would have to change some events, bringing different challenges and leading to events never considered in the first book. They would have to write a new book, not just change the ending.

I can only attest to and give according to what I know based on my experiences. Nothing more, nothing less. I hope you take what resonates and implement it in a way that helps you in your environment and circumstances. Leave out what doesn't resonate. It may help someone else. I wrote this book with that in mind. And that's at the core of Agile Parenting™. Find the elements you want to try with your child and leave those that don't apply. Agile Parenting™ is a framework, not a strict step program. And that is highly intentional.

To help you get started as a parent using the Agile Parenting™ framework, if you so choose, I am going to share with you three questions I often fall back on when I need a reset, when

I need to reconsider something in my parenting, or when I feel there is a transition period in my daughter's growth and development. I can say with absolute certainty the answers are not the ultimate answers, and they may not be your answers. They are, however, answers that work for me and my child. I am sharing these questions with you not with the expectation that you will implement them in your parenting or with the promise that they will guarantee anything if you do. I share them with you with the hope that in reading them, you may get inspired to develop your version to help you in your parenting. Because even as I have implemented my answers to these questions into my parenting, I still believe they will always be a work in progress. Also, it's perhaps that way by design. There is never one ultimate answer, but options are based on what's suitable, appropriate, considerate, kind, respectful, and simply good! Answers, much like solutions, evolve. And that is ok. Because what we need to strive for is not the ultimate; it's the iterative. The progress we make here and now. Each day. Every day. We don't want to get there before it's time to be there, which coincides with the point I make throughout this book on giving our children childhood by rethinking things like the concept of "when" in age-appropriateness.

I am not here to instruct your parenting. I am here to give you enough context to compel you to raise questions and look for answers. I am here to invite you to read the section below and invite you to reach out with constructive feedback so that together, we can try, fail fast, learn, and try some more. This connection, attitude, and parent modeling will add the most value to our children's development as individuals and as a community of emotionally and intellectually healthy people. So, dear reader, I hope you realize by now that I'm not telling you to become an Agile Parenting™ type of parent; I'm inviting you to try it. Here are the three guiding questions I use when checking in with myself as a parent and my corresponding answer.

What does parenting mean to me?

I realized parenting to mean how I experience my child and how my child experiences me. For me, it's 90% about being there to understand, not teach, guide, not direct, ask questions, not give tasks, and 10% about putting my foot down not because I am the adult and must win, but because my child's well-being and development are the center of parenting. Parenting to me is, and it always has been, about intentionality. This means I consider parenting advice coming from family and friends who are parents, but parenting advice coming from books written by experts and psychologists alike who may or may not be parents themselves is something I had decided early on was not helpful to me, especially since a lot of the findings of today will be dismissed and replaced with new findings tomorrow. Over eleven years, my thoughts on what parenting meant to me shifted focus, were modified, completely scratched out and rebooted, readjusted, ironed out, and eventually settled. Then, when I had a baby, some of what I pondered upon parenting worked, and some didn't. The important thing is I was able and willing to pivot based on what I learned about my child from my child. That's what I arrived at in answering this question for myself. Parenting to me means being alongside my child as she experiences so I can learn from her what she needs, and she learns from me what I need. Parenting to me is learning from each other (as a parent and child) and becoming each other's pillars as my child morphs from childhood to adulthood and as I morph from adulthood to elderly. Parenting is coaching, not managing. And in coaching, you are very much present at the beginning, and you slowly and gradually step back based on progress and need.

Who do I want to be as a parent?

In answering this question, I turned to experiences that have shaped who I am as an individual, how I experienced my parents as a child, and how I experienced my parents as an adult. This was where I started. This was my foundation. To that foundation, I added another component: I considered my life values and principles as an adult and how those values and principles may align or conflict with who I will and need to become as a parent. Before becoming parents, we don't think about these things. And I honestly believe we should. We need to consider at least these behind-the-scenes branches we have grown from childhood through adulthood a little before diving into becoming parents. I landed, if you will, on doing this exercise, but I think it can benefit new parents, or at least some new parents.

The short version of my answer to who I want to be as a parent is a protector of my child's childhood! Let me explain: I had a great childhood. During my childhood, I experienced my parents as strict. During adulthood, I became grateful for the parenting structure they built for my brother and me. Although in some respects I still consider my parents' approach to parenting as strict, during my infertility journey, all through my pregnancy, and after I had my child, I got a glimpse of what my child's childhood can turn into if I go along with some of the parenting approaches today. I considered it all, and my answer became apparent: as a parent, I want to make sure my child has a childhood! As a parent, I will protect and nurture my child's childhood so she doesn't grow up before her time (in my world, growing up and being mature is not the same). So, the condensed version of my answer to who I want to be as a parent is to protect my child's childhood by practicing being firm but not strict and being fully involved but not controlling.

How do I want to show up for my child?

I want to show up for my child as someone she knows will always be there for her without judging, expecting, or demanding. I want to show up for my daughter as her loving mother, as her pillar, as her friend, and as her coach. And I do this by experiencing moments with my child. I reflect on these individual moments/situations/instances and then course-correct. This is why I put a lot of effort into learning from my child what she needs versus what I think she needs, and I put a lot of effort into listening to understand my child. The way I want to show up for my child is to become and stay tuned in to her essence and provide guidance as she navigates from childhood to adulthood. I am mindful of how I want to show up for my child and pivot when she needs me to show up for her differently than how I would want someone to show up for me.

11

Evolving Together

A Framework for Intentional Parenting

I experience parenting as an enriching journey that evolves constantly with each stage of my child's development and each stage of my development as a person and parent. I believe that as long as we live, we evolve. We grow in and out of experiences and events. Yes, everyone has their path, and parenting is not on everyone's path, and that is fine. However, this book focuses on the thoughts, experiences, and perspectives I have developed over the years in my role as a parent. This doesn't mean I ignore my personal development and self-care, but being a parent is my top priority, and my day is arranged according to my child's needs first. This is not a novel idea, yet it seems like common sense for some and not easily relatable or even accepted by others. Social media doesn't help the matter.

Something I noticed over the past eight years of being a parent is overwhelmed moms making comments like, "Oh, I can't wait for school to start; I can't take it anymore with the kids at home all day, every day," or "Mommy needs mommy time." I have found myself in group conversations like these several times, and each time, I find I have nothing to add to the conversation, so I don't participate. I like it when my child is home. I miss her when she's at school. I look forward to her winter and summer breaks from school. Every year, she's excited for the first day of school, and I'm excited with her, for she will see her friends and meet new friends, but I also feel sad when I drop her off at school and come back home to a house that'll be empty for a few hours of the day. What I find interesting about these comments, such as "I can't wait for school to start so I can get some time away from my kids," is that they are not ill-meant; they are supposed to be funny. But I always feel like, what if my child hears this? Would she find such a joke of mine funny? Maybe I'm overthinking this, or perhaps I'm unwilling to be agreeable to fit in. I don't know. I get a couple of looks here and there, but I brush them off as once again being perceived as a helicopter mom, bulldozer mom, or whatever new buzzword there is for someone being categorized as "too" attached to their child. Here's the thing: I am not a perfect mom. I have made mistakes as a parent, just like I have made mistakes as an individual, and I will continue to make them. All the points I am making in this book are not to paint a picture of perfect parenting because I don't know what that would look like. It is to create awareness that we need to change the conversation on parenting. We make parenting hard these days because, on the one hand, we continue to blur the line between what children should and should not watch, do, say, and be. We don't set boundaries, or the boundaries we set are so loose they may as well not be there. On the other hand, we complain about the lack of appreciation, respect, and interest many children have for the things, people, and events in their lives. Can we have it both ways? Can we continue to blur the lines yet demand respect? What do you think? As for me, I believe that children need structure, boundaries, and proper adult modeling to learn and gain the necessary tools to help them make their own decisions and adopt their worldviews.

We all find our ways in parenting. My approach is perhaps more systematic because I had a long time to think about it, imagine it, plan it, develop it, get close to never experiencing it, experience it, and finally implement it. Because of this, most of my parenting has been highly intentional and maybe overly passionate for some.

Interestingly, I didn't even realize I was doing this kind of parenting until an opportunity presented itself in a different area of my life alongside parenting. Learning about my, at that time, newfound vocation alongside growing into what eventually became my parenting framework, which I now call AgileParenting™, I started seeing similarities in the way I was showing up in coaching teams and the way I was showing up in raising my child. I know that sounds a bit random, but it is true. And it made me think about how beneficial it has been to me to have something like a framework to lean on and consider in my parenting journey. Something like a benchmark, a base to try, modify, and build on. This is not a carefully crafted parenting framework you can plug and play. It came about unexpectedly, but it proved to be surprisingly highly functional. It has added the structure I needed to navigate better as a parent and the flexibility to adjust. Developing and using this framework over the past six years has helped me continue to shape and strengthen my relationship with my child, the most sacred of all! It has helped me build a strong relationship with my child as we both grow in and out of our similarities and differences and learn to know and understand each other's strengths and weaknesses so we can count on each other no matter how cold the external world can get. Isn't that what we all strive for as parents? I think. I hope. My life journey led me to discover and experience parenting in a somewhat uncommon yet remarkable way. Of course, that doesn't mean I haven't encountered the same challenges as any other parent, but my experience has given me a different perspective on parenting and how I make my choices as a parent. Some choose to become parents because it is the natural progression of a person's lifecycle. Others choose to become parents because it's what they want in life. Yet others see parenthood as something that happened to them while they weren't paying attention. As for me, reaching the point of becoming a parent has been one of the most excruciating, depleting, painful, and by far the most rewarding experiences of my life! My husband and I spent 11 long years knocking on that parenthood door that seemed to open for others – just not us. Still, we kept knocking until one day, we, too, were led inside. The mere length of this journey is enough to shake a person to their core. It is also a way (although not by choice) to make or break a person, which is essentially that person's choice. After years of consuming myself with this, I eventually made myself instead of breaking myself. To this day, I can't say with absolute certainty why I experienced infertility, but I do know that after everything is said and done, I feel gratitude for the pain I once found impossible to bear.

I feel gratitude for the lessons this experience led me to once I opened to receiving them. There are countless lessons I have learned and continue to learn because of this experience. These lessons help me grow and continue to shape myself as a parent and an individual with an AgileParenting™ mindset. AgileParenting™ revolves around adapting and persevering in my parental role in a manner that isn't emotionally or physically overwhelming. This approach developed from my desire to connect deeply with my child. It is based on six pillars (as described below), and it has aided me in my parenting journey, particularly in navigating the challenges of parenting in the digital era. These pillars form the core of my parenting strategy, reminding me of my reasons for parenting in my chosen style, shaping my outlook on parenting, and guiding me in reflecting on my role as a parent, filtering out external noise, and staying true to these principles in raising my child.

AgileParenting™ Pillar I: Respond to Change
One of the biggest challenges we don't pause for and spend enough time considering is how rapidly parents need to adapt to change. It's one of those things we all know goes with the territory, which is maybe why we don't pause to think about it, rather assume it's known. However, when it comes to responding and adapting to change, one size does not fit all, and not every parent is equipped for many of the challenges that come with parenting because the general notion is that "you figure it out as you go." Now, figuring it out as you go has its place in my parenting framework, but without a framework, figuring it out as I go would feel highly stressful and chaotic, much like putting out fires all the time. I find it doesn't have to be that way. Sure, there are a lot of resources for parents to turn to, but not every parent will self-initiate reaching out to any of those resources, just like not every parent will admit they may need such resources. Most parents are left to navigate parenting based on what they know, mostly modeling their parents, which can have positive and negative implications depending on many factors beyond the scope of this book's topic, aside from noting that it's never all good or bad. And that goes for anything in life. Back on topic, responding and adapting to change in my role as a parent has been easy at times yet hard at other times, but it has always been grounded in what I like to call intentional parenting – parenting on purpose, not by chance. Unfortunately, intentional parenting can be labeled a concept most parents write off as the pre-children

dreamy stage during which couples romanticize parenting that goes "out the window" once they become parents. There is some stigma attached to the whole pre and post-having-children that is widely accepted as a way to minimize or eliminate the stress and doubt in parents who feel constantly challenged in their role as a parent. The stigma has to do with how nothing can prepare you for becoming a parent, that there is this big gap between what we romanticize parenting to be versus what it is, and that once we become parents, the best we can do is make it as we go (you know… keep them alive - our children, that is). I have mixed feelings about this. I will digress here: My daughter told me the other day, while driving her to school, that she saw a book that said: "The hardest part about being a parent is kids." I asked her what she thought about that, and she said she was confused and it was making her sad. I said, *"That's interesting because I feel the best part about being a parent is you, my child!"* She sighed in relief and then mentioned having overheard some moms say they wanted to escape and be away from their kids, and that also made her feel confused and sad. I said, *"Luckily, your mom has never 'escaped' or wanted to escape from you, ever, and I'm not about to start now!"* She instantly changed her expression and said she was glad I was her mom! And that made me feel clarity and joy! I'm not going to lie; I live for these moments! Back on the stigma of parenting: I agree there isn't formal parenting training that prepares us to be parents (although, hmm… maybe that's a thought to pin…), but the make-it-as-you-go doesn't have to feel chaotic if we put effort toward intentionality in how we parent. I believe, on a societal level, we need to have a better conversation about how to parent and show up for each other as a community, especially in our digital age. There may be a plethora of information available that can be considered common sense and good practice, but how many choose to practice it? I mean, truly practice this common sense in challenging moments, in moments of vulnerability, and when all your senses are heightened because you feel everyone is staring at you and judging your next move. You only want to stop a tantrum and exit the situation immediately. Yes, the practical application of parenting is a complicated and complex undertaking, especially when you consider parenting is highly subjective and very diverse culturally and individually. Considering the individual's personality and mood at that moment, the quickest way to offend someone in the role of a parent is even remotely insinuating they are doing something wrong. We need to grow out of this. We must collectively move on from this notion that if someone says something that isn't according to our liking as a parent (and across all areas of life), the response is to lash out either actively or passive-aggressively. We need more conversations, less bickering, gossiping, and putting up a front. We need to transition into learning together, resolving differences directly with each other to grow together, not through bickering and siding. We need to allow each other to perform what I call in my parenting framework a parent-to-parent moment in retrospect. This is where I share my perspective with another parent on a given situation/topic and strictly discuss what went right and what we could improve or try next time. For this to happen, we must facilitate a safe environment for ourselves and other parents to share what they need to share without speaking back and forth. Back-and-forth speaking is when someone says something and immediately starts explaining what they meant. This is due to a need to express how we feel internally, which is immediately followed by a fear of being judged, which is a trust issue. If you say something and then almost immediately feel the need to explain what you meant, then why not just say what you meant in the first place? ... Trust.

One thing I've experienced as an observer is how much, as adults, we don't listen to each other. How much we are impatient with each other and interrupt each other in the middle of speaking just so we can get our point across and, in doing so, many times miss entirely the moment the other person was trying to make a point but was never given the time and space to make it. We are too quick to speak and mentally too distant to listen. In the realm of parenting, we need to find ways to come closer as parents and caregivers for the sake of our children. This is where I'll repeat it: it would be highly beneficial to create small community groups for parents. We could modify the education system so that these communities become an extension of each school per district. I'm not talking about the groups of parents who organize classroom parties for kids around the holidays. No, I'm talking about small groups of parents who are assigned to come together once a week after school hours to facilitate support, transfer knowledge, share ideas and resources, ask for help, connect with teachers, and have transformative conversations concerning raising our children. These groups would be structured and facilitated so they don't become social gatherings for parents, power struggles among parents, or even among parents and teachers. These groups must be highly constructive and objective and, above all, must hold space for adults to put aside all differences and unite for the greater good and well-being of our children in the digital world that continues to bring out more of the negative than the positive in both children and adults.

Children grow and change in stages. What works in one stage may not work in another. Social media adds a layer of complication that wasn't there before, and it continues to challenge us in ways that are so well packaged and marketed that it becomes harder and harder to fight against, especially for those who have already fallen into the cycle, which is a lot of people. This makes it highly challenging for parents to constantly adapt to new strategies, rules, and expectations to meet children's evolving needs, depending on their own and the parents' personalities. It requires continuous learning and adjustment. It may sound impossible, but all things considered, it seems more improbable than impossible. Why? Because of the external world we surround ourselves with through social media and all the marketing messages we are inundated with, we use scientifically proven methods and techniques to draw our attention and lock our interest in highly targeted ways, using our curiosity as a base for creating consumer-driven problems that would not otherwise exist than offer costly solutions to those problems; Solutions that are short-lived by design. We invite this into our lives whenever we reach for that electronic device. And we buy it; if not all, we buy most of it. We do this every time we absentmindedly make a peer-pressured parenting decision, feel guilty about it, and justify the action to ease the guilt, only to find ourselves in another cycle of peer-pressured parenting decision-making. We do this whenever we act in a way that aligns with the current trend of belief, movement, or latest research. Why? Why do we go along to belong? Using my AgileParenting™ framework helped me navigate through all of this and look more objectively at each distraction the external world decides to bestow upon me and my child in a way that keeps me sane in my parenting approach.

AgileParenting™ Pillar II: Practice Consistency

While flexibility plays a vital role in parenting, I find it equally important, if not more important, to be consistent with rules, discipline, and routines to provide a stable environment for my child. Balancing flexibility with structure is a challenge that can persist and slowly create a sense of guilt and resentment if such balance is not reached. I am fully aware of this, so I believe the key to practicing consistency is understanding that consistency is not aiming at perfection but practice. It requires discerning when to stand firm and when to flex. It's not about reinforcing rules and discipline every single time. It's also not about bending rules and discipline according to convenience. It's about recognizing when discipline is called for and when an instance can be just that. This is easier said than done, especially if there isn't some framework to guide parents during times of overwhelm, which is when it's the hardest to achieve consistency. One of the most important things to me is to be completely transparent and honest with myself as a parent. I set a framework to guide myself through moments I feel most challenged in my role as a parent. Consistency is one of the critical challenges of parenting because it requires us to well... be consistent. When asked about consistency in parenting, I always bring up the analogy that parenting is not and cannot be a sidekick. It's a full-time job that needs to be considered as such! Not by lip service but by actions. I entered parenting with that understanding. Whatever the circumstances, when parenting happens, it's a blessing—the biggest one. We must treat it as such during low moments just as much as during high moments. Our children are not burdens that need to be managed. They don't turn mean and ungrateful overnight. They are toward us the way we are toward them. This is one way I do my check-in with myself as a parent. I pay close attention to my child's behavior, and when I notice a change, I first reflect on my behavior (in the past week or month) and make sure I put the effort into my course correction. If I don't find anything in my self-reflection, I start asking my daughter clarifying questions so she can help me understand what's behind her behavior. Sometimes there is something there, and we talk about it, and sometimes there is nothing specific, just a bad day. That's OK, too. We acknowledge it, and we leave it at that. For some, this may sound exhausting and maybe even unnecessary. For me, it is crucial. Who's right and who's wrong? I couldn't tell you, but it works great for my child and me and is part of the AgileParenting™ framework. My AgileParenting™ framework keeps me consistent with my words and actions in building a meaningful relationship with my child. Imagine how cool it would be if each parent had another parent as an accountability partner to help do check-ins and course corrections regularly. To clarify, to be done correctly, an accountability partner is not one of your friends. It's someone who you connect with for the sole purpose of keeping you or each other accountable. This approach could work great in schools where parents who do not know each other otherwise can be paired up and set up regular accountability partnership calls or meet-ups.

AgileParenting™ Pillar III: Regulate Emotions

Navigating through tantrums, defiance, and the array of emotions children display can test a parent's patience and emotional resilience. Learning to manage my feelings in the face of stress is a continual challenge on both a personal level and in my role as a parent. Everyone experiences emotions differently and responds to triggers differently. A big part of regulating our emotions is how clear and robust our why is as individuals and in our role as parents. This is key. Again, it's never about being a perfect parent; it's always about being a growing parent. We learn and grow as children. Then, we learn and grow with our children. It's a beautiful concept if you let it be. I am not a perfect parent, but I am a growing parent. I fully understand that not everything I firmly believe to be suitable for my child will be fully appreciated by her. That's OK.

Every day, we learn from each other and readjust. Sometimes, readjusting means being more flexible, yet other times, it means practicing our parent-child "power" ratio. The one constant thing is open, transparent, thorough, and consistent communication (there is that consistency thing again). Consistent communication has allowed my child to know that her thoughts, emotions, and ideas are valid and always included in our decision-making process at home with the clear understanding that we (my husband and I) are the parents and have the final word. We take care that the final word is according to our values as a family, our duty as part of a community, and what's in our child's best interest. At times, our final word is something that stretches our likes and dislikes as parents and helps our daughter learn through her own experiences, but it's always within our values and principles. It's a lot of work. And sometimes it feels easy to say: "Because I said so." I've done it. My husband has done it. The important part is to take a deep breath, reset, admit to the shortcomings, and course-correct. Why? If I keep doing this as a parent and my husband keeps doing this as a parent, our child will start modeling a similar path as she builds meaningful relationships with people outside our home. So yeah, is it repetitive, challenging, and, at times, nauseatingly annoying to keep going through the course-correcting exercise? Yes. Yes, it is. Am

I going to keep at it regardless of judging hearts and whispering comments? Yes, yes, I am! I will even continue volunteering to help parents open to receiving and considering thoughts, ideas, and suggestions that differ from what they may or may not have considered themselves in exchange for thoughts, ideas, and tips I haven't considered. Like I said, I'm not a perfect parent; I'm a growing parent willing and able to pivot if it's in my child's and my family's best interest. That's how genuinely supportive communities of parents can form. One small act of kindness and support at a time, away from text messages and comments on virtual social platforms.

AgileParenting™ Pillar IV: Making Time
Most parents juggle the demands of parenting with work, personal time, and relationships. Finding the time to cater to each child's needs feels like a never-ending competition, with the chances of winning becoming slimmer with each round. One of the main reasons time management can become a real struggle with parents is that not all parents have access to a strong support network, such as extended family or reliable childcare options. This lack of support can make it even more challenging to manage time effectively, so we need to take a step back and rethink our view on parenting as part of the whole picture in our society. The disconnect we experience on a societal level is that we look at each role we play as a separate compartment. We are siloed in our own lives. We work in silos in all areas of life, with each silo shooting out its requirements and demands that are very different and require different levels of energy that we have limited amounts of in a day. For many, the concept of work-life balance is so far-fetched to the point it becomes comical. How is it that even after all the technological progress and productivity

tools and gadgets we have created, time management remains in a deficit?

We continue to report not having enough hours in the day, not enough days in the week, just not enough time for all the responsibilities we need to tend to daily. We are not focusing on fundamental, on-purpose changes that bring value to the actual quality of life, not a perceived quality of life. No matter what stage in life we are in, current societal values dictate we must chase after our dreams, our ambitions, and all the things we "deserve." Because if we don't, we've fallen behind. And no matter how many books have already been written about how unsustainable and unhealthy this way of thinking is, we continue to buy into and fall for the don't-fall-behind trap. We seem to continue to fight time management, yet we cannot achieve such a balance in our daily operations. A state of being where we have finally conquered time and are now managing it so we can fit all our dreams, ambitions, and all the things we've been chasing. Where does raising our children fall in this chase? I often wonder why this is a thing. Why are we after everything we are after?

We sure were not born with all this baggage. We collected it along the way and can't seem to unload it. Why? Observing my child through the different stages in her development (so far), I can tell you she's not worried about any of these "things," not because she's a child, but because we talk about the "things," and we talk about the importance of recognizing our needs and being selective with our wants based on purpose and functionality, not based on recognition, prizes, and a mindset founded on more is better. I love having these discussions with my eight-year-old. I get inspired by her as we both learn from each other. What I hope for, the reason behind building this kind of parenting framework for myself and my child and parenting through this framework for the past six years and going, is to set the foundation for her to not fall for all the distractions society increasingly poses upon us to keep us occupied. Instead, I hope to set the foundation for her to maintain her navigation system and stand still as she watches all kinds of distractions from the external world bounce off and fade away from her.

AgileParenting™ Pillar V: Navigate Social Pressures
From basic needs to education to extracurricular activities, as parents, we often must make tough decisions about where to allocate our resources. Some parents find themselves in a continuous survival mode and can't seem to improve their financial circumstances, no matter how hard their efforts are. Society makes it harder and harder to define and separate necessity from luxury, especially with everything being available and accessible faster and earlier in life. Children being provided with electronic devices from an earlier and earlier age in the name of safety and somewhat educational exposure adds to the financial stress of a parent who struggles to make ends meet and, on top of it, feels guilty for not being able to provide their children with a device that is seemingly keeping them safer and more intelligent. Never mind that most of these devices come with a plentitude of features used for entertainment purposes and impose a level of distraction children should be shielded from, not exposed to. There are many extracurricular activities parents today feel obligated to do just so their child doesn't feel like an outsider, but they all cost, and the prices continue to rise. Is a once-a-week ballet class for a three-year-old worth $150 per month? Sure, it's only $37.50 per class, but is it only? What if you have three different activities you are taking your child to? What if you have three or more children?

You do the math. Yes, they are optional, and you could go with the theory that if you can't afford it, you don't do it, but how many parents are practicing this instead of killing themselves to make enough to be able to get their children to these activities so they don't feel like they are missing out? Extracurricular activities are a choice. However, there is a peer-pressure component to these activities, which is taken advantage of in the cost of those activities. It is unfair to push consumerism through carefully crafted emotional cues and accept no responsibility in the aftermath of such actions. We all need to take responsibility and help each other. We must stop dividing and unite as communities to help each other meaningfully. Making monetary donations or even collecting things for donations is an approach that adds to the class division and amplifies the gap. Connecting families in need with families in excellent financial standing where knowledge transfer and peer support through coaching can be facilitated to help a family get on their feet is a great way to "donate." We need to think about donating through collaboration and volunteering to spend time with people within our small communities and help each other with resources, knowledge, training, etc., so they can start making sustainable, self-sufficient improvements.

AgileParenting™ Pillar VI: Mitigate Self-Doubt

As parents, we may sometimes feel inadequacy or self-doubt, wondering if we are making the right decisions for our child's well-being and future. Overcoming these challenges requires a mix of resilience, patience, support, and love. It's essential for parents to seek out resources, support groups, or counseling when needed and to remember that it's OK to ask for help. This is assuming parents are open to it. The challenge is that not every parent is open to these resources or comfortable with self-initiating them. At least not until there is an absolute need and the circumstances can no longer be patched or ignored. This is not a healthy way to be and function and is even more unhealthy for children to be around and experience. No matter how good a parent is at covering issues, children are more intelligent than we give them credit for and a lot more intuitive – they can sense our troubles. Self-doubt can result from many different life experiences and circumstances as children and into adulthood that spill over into our parenting and have the potential to spiral off. The idea is to address the challenges before they become problems. The idea is to prevent a meltdown. Simply telling someone to contact all these resources isn't helpful and can feel forced. We need to support each other as individuals, neighbors, colleagues, friends, and relatives by making time for face-to-face conversations that happen often and are honest. Conversations that are not just verbally supportive but action-based. How can we build trust and help each other in ways that display genuine kindness, fairness, honesty, transparency, and emotional and mental lift for our children to model? How about building communities of parents around a framework that supports and encourages all these things among adults and becomes a mindset and a tool for our children to continue to build on and grow with?

12

Parenting on Purpose

The Essence of Active Parenting

Bonding with my child is the most important thing for me as a parent. This is a central theme in the Agile Parenting™ platform. The bonding period can look and feel different for each parent and child and for each parent with each child they have. If you have five children, your bonding will most likely be different with each child, but this doesn't affect the strength of the bond. The crucial aspect of meaningful bonding is being actively present with each child.

When my daughter was an infant, she did not like being in her bassinet for some reason. When I put her down, she would wake up and want to be picked up. As soon as I would pick her up, she would stop crying. Now, I've heard what parenting books direct you to do – to let the baby cry, letting the baby know it's okay to be on their own – I failed that. Instead, I picked my baby up and held her in my arms. I would often walk around the house holding her in my arms and singing to her (in my beautiful voice) or talking to her. She would look at me for a while as though she understood every word I said (she didn't) and even throw a smile (the baby-adorable kind of smile that melts your soul), and then she would fall asleep.

At that point, I would continue to walk around the house and talk to her for a bit longer before sitting on the couch and putting her right next to me or holding her while reading a book so I wouldn't fall asleep with her. Eight years later, I can report my child does not struggle with independence. Bonding this way was the first stage in building a relationship with my child. I continue to develop that relationship every day. I held my daughter in my arms, putting her crib next to my bed for the first six months, waking up in the middle of the night to pick her up when she cried for her mommy, and staying with her for as long as she needed me, or even taking her with me in our bed some nights when I was so tired I just had to lie down so I would put her right next to me while my husband would sleep in the guest room so he could get up for work in the morning. These are all the ways I failed much of the advice and many of the recommendations of the books on parenting I never bothered to read. And I would do it all over again! This is probably just me (not), but the first eight years of my child's life went by so fast it makes me want to cry just thinking about it. But I find solace in knowing I spent maximum time with her during those years. Many times, I've been a conversation piece (and I'm no gem, I'll tell you that) for spending too much time with my child, for not taking time for myself, for making her too dependent on me (I couldn't if I tried to), for not getting out much (I think I got out quite enough in my 20's and I don't miss it), for basing my schedule too much on my child's schedule, etc. The list can go on and on. To all of that, I have no comment other than I keep doing it repeatedly and have no intention of stopping! Yes, I have opted out of many plans, events, and parties that were not child-friendly, and there hasn't been a single time that I have regretted choosing my child over a few hours of party time.

Another important thing to me as a parent is holding space for my child to express her thoughts and emotions. Bonding with her made her feel safe, and she started forming her center on a strong ground. Building on that concept, I felt I needed to create the space for her to feel comfortable sharing her thoughts and emotions with me and know that I will always tell her the truth because the truth will always lead her to the right answer(s) so she can make choices that are right for her and never at the cost of someone else. This part involves many, and I mean many, long discussions (or, as my daughter would more accurately call them, "loooooooooooong" talks). I take every opportunity I can to have those talks with my child. Full transparency: Currently, I am re-evaluating my long talk approach as I've been using it for a while, and I can tell my child's responsiveness toward these talks is changing. I feel she's no longer interested when I go on a topic for a while. Great, point taken, lesson in the learning; I want to modify my approach. I'll let you know what I come up with if I figure it out before finishing this book. This is a good segue-way to another point I want to share with you before I return to the next most important thing in building a relationship with my child. Parenting is one big trial and error. Many people say nothing can prepare you for being a parent. This is usually followed by commenting on the demands children pose. These comments are intended to be funny – and they are funny – but they are also a bit overdone. They are meant to be relatable and help us find a sense of ease through humor, knowing parenting is hard for everyone. Although there is a good amount of truth in this, I will argue that we contribute to the very complaints we express about parenting. We may even be instigating a lot of the behavior in our children. How? First, by making these harmless, funny comments in front of them, we validate their behavior so they continue to act that way. Second, exposing children to social media content far too early makes it easy for the external world to take over and become the source of modeling behavior for our children. Third, by keeping up with the times and providing for our children according to what society puts before us, we endorse and feed our children the idea that they don't need to think and all they need to do is follow along with society. Giving children access to everything at once, including content, merchandise, language, and pop culture, beyond what's appropriate for their age, robs them of their natural opportunity to experience childhood. It shortens their childhood as they are thrown from infancy to puberty far too quickly. This is so sad to watch; it feels like there isn't much one can do. I can't write it off as 'growing with the times' and 'kids are smarter today than we were.' I'm not sure how a toddler who knows how to operate a smartphone but cannot register the word 'no' is smart. A five-year-old dancing in a provocative way copied from the latest pop-culture icon video that the five-year-old somehow got access to is not cute; it's worrisome. In a society that wants us to believe in equality, we continue to encourage and normalize the sexualization of the female body and accept the filming of little girls doing some of these moves and posting those videos as a form of entertainment is wrong even though in many instances it is not ill-meant. No, dear reader, I will not chill about this. I stand firm when I say we must rethink what we expose our children to and at what age. My daughter knew nothing about any pop-culture celebrity or icon until she turned seven and started first grade. I find that tragicomic. She didn't miss out on anything, anything important, that is. In fact, "missing out" on a lot of the content most of the kids at her school seem to have already been exposed to has provided room for her to ask intelligent questions to help herself process information much more maturely. And this is how it works in our household. She asks questions, and we have discussions that help her decide if what the kids at school are talking about or are into is something she would choose to join or observe from a safe distance. And that is all I ask for. I want my child to think with her mind and not be pressured, shamed, or easily fall into traps intentionally and inadvertently coming her way. I know I can't always be next to her; I know she will make decisions I will not agree with; I know she will make mistakes she could've prevented if she listened to me in the first place. That is all fine. But none of it is a reason for me to be a passive onlooker in her life, claiming I'm giving her the freedom to be independent and express herself. Giving my child a childhood is what I am accountable for as a parent, and that means I need to be actively involved in her life as a child. When the time comes, she will have the things she comes from school telling me other kids already have (it normally involves electronic gadgets or access to apps or certain TV shows). She doesn't need a TikTok profile, a Messenger account, or a phone used as a constant entertainment source on the go. The difference is that when she has access to these things, she will already have the foundation to know how to use them responsibly and be selective in deciding what deserves her time and attention and what can be written off as background noise.

Another important thing to me as a parent is listening to understand my child, not to solve everything for her. Listening to someone to understand their point(s) requires a temporary disregard for everything around me but the person I am holding space for – kind of like noise cancellation – especially when that person is my child. Children are very much what I like to call tuned in. They can tell if you are paying attention to them or are there to fill space. They don't always know how to articulate that and often will bluntly call you on it. For example, I try to do my best not to be engaged in anything else when my child is trying to tell me something. If I am already engaged in something and I'm not able to stop and drop, I don't try to multitask; I tell her to give me a minute, or two, or five to wrap up what I am doing or get to a stopping point, so I can then, pay full attention to her. I stick with that, stop when the time is up, and give her my full attention. In one instance, I was reading an article on my phone that I needed for a presentation I had the next day at work. My daughter started telling me something. It didn't require an urgent response, but it was a matter she felt she wanted to share with me at that time (I can't remember what it was). I didn't stop and drop, and I didn't tell her to give me a minute or pause with my article. Instead, I split my attention between what I was reading and what she was trying to tell me. She was not used to this. So, she stopped in the middle of her talking and said: "Can you listen to me?". I shook my head like I was out of a trance. Wait, what? My child called me out for being on my phone?? I don't do that. I talk a lot about not being that person, and now I'm being called out for acting like that person. It was like a dagger in my heart! It still rings in my ears every time I think about it. It was also a great lesson as it reminded me of how easy it is to give in to daily happenings and get pulled in different directions all day long and how much more important it is to be intentional in parenting. In that instance, I was not being intentional. I dropped the ball. And that's okay. Not because what I was doing was okay, but because, by practicing my Agile Parenting™ framework, I could turn that instance into a lesson and use that lesson never to make that same mistake again. Maybe make a different mistake, but not that one! What I love about this instance is that I don't feel ashamed for dropping the ball like that. I feel a sense of pride. My child taught me a lesson, making me proud of her. That she felt comfortable enough to call me out on something I was doing wrong; that through being intentional with my parenting, I can count on my child calling me out on things just like I call her out on things so we can learn from each other and grow an inch better each day. That instance was a great lesson because it felt like a slap in the face. Luckily, sometimes I'm a fast learner, so my daughter doesn't have to repeat that lesson with me again! Always listen to understand. As part of listening to understand, I intentionally let her finish talking and always ask follow-up questions. This tells her that she is heard and that I am interested in what she is telling me. I am engaged in her story, her experience, and her thoughts. It sets an atmosphere where she can feel comfortable enough to ask for advice or come back with additional questions for me and keep a conversation going. This is so important for children to learn – how to start and maintain a conversation – and use as they enter their teenage years and adulthood. It all starts from childhood. Another important thing to me as a parent is guidance over teaching. During the early months with my child, while observing every move she made, I planned about everything I would teach her. But then, one day, it hit me: I don't want to teach her anything per se. I want to give her what she needs, and teaching her would give her what I think she needs. As a rather independent child myself, I remember how much I didn't like to be taught; I remember how much I wanted to learn on my own, which in a sense explains why I never liked school, but I loved, and I still am in love with, learning about things I'm interested in. It hit me at that moment that it would be much more beneficial to my child if I let her teach me what she is interested in learning. A great realization, I thought to myself, but how do I do that? After all, I am the adult, the parent, and she needs to learn from me. I didn't know how to make this happen, so I set it aside to revisit later. A couple of years later, the answer presented itself. What I couldn't figure out before was that I wanted to guide my child through her childhood, not necessarily drive her childhood. To guide her, I would need to be very much present throughout her childhood (not that that was ever a question). So interestingly enough, what the external world saw as me being a helicopter mother or a bulldozing mother, I was navigating alongside my child. I refrain from telling my child to do this, not that, and end it there. It's always a question: Do you think this is something you should do or not do? Followed by: Why? Then, I would offer my answer to the same questions and my reasoning to decide on a final answer together. I understand that, as written, this sounds like a long-drawn-out process (who has the time to do this every single time?), but the truth is we can't afford not to do this; I know I can't, and I wouldn't. It's too important in the world we live in today for one parent (preferably the mother) to be the main pillar, stay home with their child/children, and engage in intentional parenting without feeling a negative impact on the family financially or otherwise. As a stay-at-home parent, you should be able to have these moments with your child/children without being overwhelmed or physically exhausted from trying to make ends meet. Our society/culture/establishment should be able to support this. Again, we are far from where we need to be on this topic, so we must spend more time and resources figuring this out. It's overdue, and it's ridiculous that in the name of moving with the times, we let important human values and ethics become less and less relevant. Let's change that. Let's start now!

Agile **Parenting**
FRAMEWORK

workbook

Why This Workbook

Parenting is both rewarding and challenging. With a clear purpose and a well-established navigation system, you can tame the difficulties and enhance the joys. This workbook provides a framework to discover your guiding principles and apply them to your parenting approach by creating a plan of action. This plan is not about treating parenting as a project with a start and end date—parenting is an ongoing journey. Instead, it aims to add structure to help you navigate the ups and downs of parenthood. The plan of action acts as a guide, keeping you aligned with your best self. In an uncertain world, the only constant is that we are all works in progress. Why not define for ourselves what that progress looks and feels like? This workbook offers one way to do that. It's up to you to give it a try or pass it by.

* * *

Instructions

- **Agile Parenting™ Framework Visual:**

    This workbook begins with a visual representation of my Agile Parenting™ Framework. The framework is built around three essential questions that every parent should take the time to thoughtfully consider. Additionally, it includes six areas, each with three guiding principles, designed to help you create your personalized agile parenting roadmap.

- **Self Discovery Workbook:**

    Following the Agile Parenting™ Framework visual, you'll find the main content of the workbook. This section requires your focused effort, so I recommend setting aside dedicated time for this work. Here are two effective approaches:

    - Treat it like a one-day seminar: Set aside eight uninterrupted hours to fully immerse yourself in the work.
    - Break it down into sections: Allocate two hours of distraction-free time per section. This approach adds more total time but includes buffer periods for each section, allowing you to settle in and focus on deep work. Don't rush through the questions; this is not about speed but about giving yourself the necessary time to engage with each part of the workbook. Some people need over 30 minutes just to get into the right mindset for this kind of work. Take that time and be patient.

Instructions

- **Your Agile Parenting™ Roadmap:**

  After completing the workbook and writing your action plan, you'll have a template of the framework where you get to set principles you want to focus on in each of the six areas of the Agile Parenting™ Framework. Use this visual in your daily life. Keep it somewhere visible to you and your family. Make it a fun journey toward your optimal parenting approach by involving your children and encouraging their support along the way.

- **The Three Fundamental Questions:**

  Once you've established your own Agile Parenting™ principles, keep the three fundamental questions in mind as you apply your work in practice. These questions will help you regain focus whenever you get off track, which you will; We all have fallen off-track The goal is not to perfect your parenting approach but to have a reliable support system and techniques you can draw from and regroup.
  This workbook lays the foundation for activating your support system. It requires 8-10 hours of dedicated work, a commitment to taking ownership of your situation, and a willingness to experience short-term discomfort for long-term gain.

table of contents

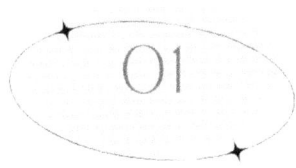

Ideal
You will start by defining your ideal approach to parenting. You will hold on to this idea in your mind as you navigate through the questions in this section building a bridge to the next section.

Current Reality
In this section you will dive into your current reality in your parenting approach to help you establish an internal center and become comfortable with where you are before moving to the next milestone in building your roadmap.

Focus
Once you have established your internal center you are ready to zoom-in to the emotional challenge that you consider top priority at this time. In this section you will assess your relationship with this challenge.

Connect
Here you will start by reviewing your work this far. Then you will have a space to explore your own mindset, so take your time. You may surprise yourself. Finally, you will arrive at your parenting baseline. This is the crossroad.

Action
It's time to act. Here, you will put all your effort into a tangible, actionable, and measurable roadmap you will implement in your parenting approach and use on daily basis. This is your navigation system toward your ideal parenting. Do not set it aside for later. It's for now!

Ideal

Q1:
What does your parenting approach look and feel like if you disregard your current personal and parenting challenges?

Q2:
What does your parenting approach look and feel like now (in face of your challenges)?

Q3:
Considering your current parenting challenges, what would you say is a **reasonable progress** toward your ideal parenting approach? Pick between 1-3 main areas/points. What does progress in those 1-3 areas/points look and feel like?

Q4:
What would you have to give up to make reasonable progress and keep **progressing toward you ideal**? How difficult would it be to give it up? How willing are you to give it up?

Q5:
What is stopping you (thoughts, feelings, events, people...) from taking the first step toward becoming the parent you envision yourself to become?

Reality

Q1:
List your emotions as they relate to your current parenting approach.

Q2:
If you were to single out one emotion from your list above, as the most persistent of all, which one would it be?

Q3:
What have you tried to help you release this emotion or at least minimize it in intensity and frequency?

Q4:
Is it possible what you are doing now is one or more of the following:
- Not truly helping?
- Standing in the way of something potentially better?
- Taking you away from what you ultimately want?

First, give a yes or no answer to each question, then go back and answer why or why not.

Q5:
If you decide to revisit your current parenting approach and find you are open to try something slightly different, what would that be? What would you start with? In what order?

Focus

Q1:
What is the most emotionally challenging thing/event about your parenting approach?

Elaborate. The more details the better.

Q2:
Keeping in mind what's most emotionally challenging for you as a parent answer the following:

- How do you feel about your most emotionally challenging thing as a parent?

- How do you feel about addressing it?

- How reasonable is it to address it in this way?

- How rational is it to address it in this way?

- What will happen if you address it in this way?

- Does addressing it this way take care of the challenge or the emotions associated with the challenge?

- Do you truly believe this is the only way of addressing it?

- What are some other possibilities to address this challenge?

Connect

Review the following:

1. Go back to **Ideal**. Read your answers. Pay close attention to your **answers to questions 1-4**.
2. Go back to **Focus**. Read your **answer to question 1**.
3. Go back to **Reality**. Read **answer to question 2**.

Then...

Write the answers to the questions below and compare to your progression of events leading to your **reasonable progress**.
- Do you feel you are making progress in getting to your ideal parenting approach?
- What is that progress?
- What do you think about your progress? Is it fast? Slow?
- Does this kind of progress offer grounding? In what way?

Then...

Write the answers to the questions below and compare to your progression of events leading to your **ideal parenting approach**.
- Is it the best advice you would give to someone you tremendously care about?
- Are you willing to change anything about your approach to parenting based on your progress?
- Are you willing to explore this new approach deeper? How?

Connect

The following section is designed to help you capture your essence using questions as guiding principles. Feel free to write, draw, color, paint, or use whatever medium your heart desires to unlock the door to what is going to become your own guiding principles as a parent.

- What do you consider threatening to your well being and safety?
- What is your autopilot response to situations you find threaten your general well being and safety?
- What does being part of a whole look like to you? What would your part be in it?
- In this whole (as you envision it), how valuable are your connections/relationships with those around you?
- What would you do and to what extent would you go to ensure your whole is untamed?
- What gives you a sense of self-worth?
- How important is it to you to maintain a sense of self-worth? Why?
- What is the extent to which you would go to ensure your self-worth is apparent to you and to those around you? *Elaborate.*
- What do you do when you are presented with countless number of options or potential solutions to a challenge?
- What do you do when you are presented with only one option or potential solutions to a challenge? *Elaborate.*
- Do you find yourself in a constant state of seeking new experiences or learning new things? *Elaborate.*
- Is the World a playground to be forever explored or is it a work-field to be maintained, fixed, improved?

Connect

Go back to the questions you just worked on and review your answers. Use the dot grid space for notes to help you **rate the information by its importance** as it relates to your present self – your life right now.

Note

You can use different concepts to conduct the rating process. For example, you can rate each answer on a scale of 1-10 (1=not important; 10=extremely important); Or
you can number each question in the order of it's importance; Or
you can color each page by its intensity in relevance to your present self.

Remember

- **This is not a placement test.**
- It is a self discovery test.
- You chose what you include on the pages and how you rate the pages. <u>The only constriction is that your final result is having the pages rated from most important to least important.</u>

Connect

Findings

The information you rated highest in importance, based on your rating system, is your baseline. Below are two sets of actions you have turned into habits that either prevent you from living according to your guiding , or help you be in sync with it. Circle the ones you find yourself doing most in each set.

There is one caveat to this: YOU MUST BE HONEST. If you truly want to move forward from your present enigma. Use the dotted space to write down instances you find yourself utilizing the actions/habits you circled.

Set 1
- criticizing
- blaming
- complaining
- nagging
- threatening
- pushing
- bribing/rewarding

Set 2
- supporting
- encouraging
- listening
- accepting
- trusting
- respecting
- negotiating differences

Before moving on the final step make sure:
- By now you are open and willing to do this kind of work.
- You are clear on what your baseline is and you are welcoming of it, even if you don't quite understand its full impact on your well being as you move forward.
- You have identified one action/habit from each set that you choose to improve on.
- You are clear on everything you have worked on so far.

Action

- What are you willing to do differently?
- How do you plan to go about your different approach to parenting?
- Time to create your plan of action: create it in a way that
  - Makes sense to you,
  - Encourages you to keep it close to heart - close to mind, but most of all:
    - **Inspires you to follow and stick to it!**

Your Plan of Action

To be powerful, practical, and actionable your action plan needs to clearly:

State your baseline.

Describe how your baseline relates to your current mindset on parenting.

Identify your current actions/habits you chose to improve and why.

State how you will go about implementing your new actions/habits.

Describe current situations you find challenging.

List your **current actions** upon experiencing each challenging situation.

List your choice of **new actions** to replace each old action every time you experience a situation you find challenging.

Agile Parenting
FRAMEWORK

In the following pages, refine the action plan you created with the workbook by aligning your information with the Agile Parenting™ Framework. Consider how your baseline integrates within this framework. What does it look like, feel like, and sound like? This process will help you develop your personalized parenting roadmap. Use this roadmap to navigate the highs and lows of parenting, guiding you toward the direction you have defined and chosen for yourself as both a parent and an individual.

You can use the bullet points to add your information from your action plan. For example, what is your "Respond to Change" in the Change door? How will you choose to respond to change based on your baseline? In other words, what would you replace the "Listen to Understand" bullet point with? What action will you practice to go to automatically?

Once you have your Agile Parenting™ roadmap, it's essential to integrate it into your daily routine. Here are some practical ways to help you stay aligned with your parenting goals:

- **Print it out and display it:** Place a printed copy in a location where you'll see it every day.
- **Digital reminders:** Set it as the background image on your digital devices to keep it in sight each time you use them.
- **Carry a hard copy:** Keep a physical copy in your bag for easy reference.
- **Focus using individual cards:** Print out each area or door as individual cards, allowing you to concentrate on one aspect at a time.
- **Involve your children:** Engage your child or children as accountability partners, navigating the roadmap together. This collaborative approach can be enjoyable and helps everyone stay on track. Remember, the process might be challenging initially, but that's part of the journey toward improvement. Embrace the concept of "fail fast, then pivot, and try again."

By consistently socializing and revisiting your roadmap, you'll ensure that it becomes an integral part of your parenting approach.

Agile Parenting
FRAMEWORK

What does parenting mean to me

Who do I want to be as a parent

How do I want to show up for my child

Change
- Make it as you go, intentionally.
- Listen to understand.
- Evolve through parent-to-parent.

Respond to Change

Emotions
- Grow out of perfection.
- Learn through open dialogue.
- Course-correct.

Regulated Emotions

Social
- Offer help/ask for help.
- Exit virtual social.
- Enter real-time conversations.

Social Pressure Navigation

Consistency
- Balance flexibility & structure.
- Align with self-honesty.
- Reflect on your parenting.

Consistency Practice

- Build a support network.
- Choose purpose and functionality.
- Release distractions.

Making Time

Self-Doubt
- Prevent instead of treat.
- Grow with your child.
- Grow with your community.

Alleviated Self-Doubt

Agile **Parenting**
FRAMEWORK

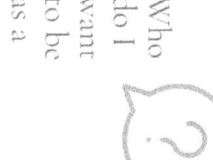

What does parenting mean to me

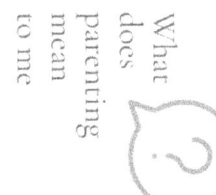

Who do I want to be as a parent

How do I want to show up for my child

Social

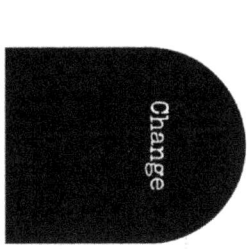

Emotions

Change

.... Social Pressure Navigation

.... Regulated Emotions

.... Respond to Change

Self-Doubt

Time

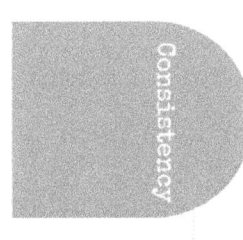

Consistency

.... Alleviated Self-Doubt

.... Making Time

.... Consistency Practice

Agile **Parenting** ROADMAP

? What does parenting mean to me

? Who do I want to be as a parent

? How do I want to show up for my child

Thank you for reading.

What could be next?

Scan the code below to choose one or more of the following three options as you continue on this journey.

1.
You are welcome to check out my **Coaching by Bia** website and reach out to me directly to explore ways we can work together.

2.
You can follow my new **Agile Parenting Facebook page**, where you can get updates and initiate and participate in engaging conversations.

3.
You are welcome to join my newly created private **Agile Parents Facebook group** (check out my Agile Parenting Facebook page), where you can initiate a conversation with a small group of parents.

www.ingramcontent.com/pod-product-compliance
Lightning Source LLC
Chambersburg PA
CBHW051618010526
44119CB00008B/190